Copenhagen Travel Guide

What You Should Know Before Traveling To Copenhagen; Brief History Of Copenhagen; Where To Stay And Getting Around; Must Do Things; Copenhagen Christmas Markets; Copenhagen For Solo Travelers; Samples Of Planned Itineraries

GW00481011

Steve K. Bonds

Copenhagen

Table of Contents

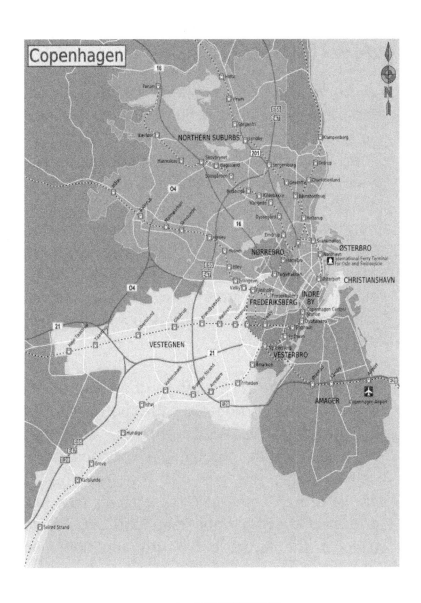

Map Of Copenhagen

INTRODUCTION

Welcome to the vibrant pages of our comprehensive Copenhagen travel guide book. As you open these chapters, you're opening a door to a city that seamlessly weaves its rich history into the fabric of modern life. From its medieval origins and regal architecture to its trendsetting design and sustainable initiatives, Copenhagen is a tapestry of experiences waiting to be explored. Join us as we delve into the maze of charming streets, navigate the intricate canals, and unravel the stories that have shaped this dynamic capital.

Whether you're captivated by the allure of the Little Mermaid, enticed by the mouthwatering delights of New Nordic cuisine, or simply seeking to wander through the cozy nooks that define hygge, this guide is your compass to navigate the depths of Copenhagen's past and present. So, grab your map and set out to uncover the layers of culture, tradition, and innovation that make this city truly one of a kind.

COPENHAGEN

DENMARK

Do you know that;

- One of the safest cities in the world is Copenhagen.
- Copenhageners have a religion of cycling!
- One of the greenest cities in the world right now is Copenhagen.
- Copenhagen boasts the world's greatest metro system, and the workplaces there are highly pleasant.
- A Copenhagen neighborhood has its flag and money.
- Copenhagen is where the Danish royal family resides.
- You can swim in Copenhagen Harbor since it is so pristine.
- Copenhagen was formerly a fishing community.
- Copenhagen served as the capital of Denmark as well as Sweden and Norway.
- Swedish prisoners of war dug the renowned Nyhavn canal.
- The pandemic has decimated Copenhagen.

- Copenhagen is where the renowned Carlsberg Brewery was established.
- One of the world's longest pedestrian retail districts is accessible by foot.
- Sweden may be reached in less than 40 minutes from Copenhagen.
- It's a bustling city with a flourishing arts community.
- There are at least 15 Michelin-starred restaurants in Copenhagen.
- Copenhagen is a design temple.
- The city's emblem is The Little Mermaid.
- The author of The Little Mermaid resides in Nyhavn
- Children are highly valued in Copenhagen.
- One of the world's oldest theme parks is located in Copenhagen.
- Since 1980, Copenhagen has had its marathon.

Do you know that there are Free things you can do in Copenhagen? Check the list below and enjoy your vacation in Copenhagen

- Tivoli Gardens
- Superkilen park
- Copenhagen City Hall
- Designmuseum Denmark
- Frederiksberg Park
- Strøget
- Rosenborg Castle
- Botanical Garden
- National Museum of Denmark
- Christiansborg Palace
- Ny Carlsberg Glyptotek
- Amalienborg Palace
- Nyhavn
- Christiania
- The Little Mermaid
- Torvehallerne
- Kastellet
- Kongens Have
- The David Collection
- Church of Our Saviour
- National Gallery of Denmark
- Thorvaldsens Museum
- Bakken

Chapter 1: Brief History Of Copenhagen

Medieval Origins and Renaissance (10th - 16th Century): Copenhagen's history traces back to the Viking Age, when it began as a small fishing village. In the 12th century, Bishop Absalon fortified the settlement and constructed a castle, marking the birth of Copenhagen. Throughout the Middle Ages, the city's strategic location on the Øresund strait facilitated trade and maritime activities, contributing to its growth.

In the 15th century, Copenhagen became the capital of Denmark and experienced urban development. The University of Copenhagen was founded in 1479, solidifying the city's status as a center of learning and culture. Landmarks like the Round Tower (Rundetårn) and Rosenborg Castle (Rosenborg Slot) were built during this period.

Trade and Enlightenment (17th - 18th Century): The 17th century witnessed Copenhagen's rise as a trading powerhouse, thanks in part to the establishment of the Danish East India Company. The city flourished as a global trading hub, and its maritime activities brought wealth and cultural exchange.

In 1801 and 1807, Copenhagen was besieged by the British navy due to Denmark's alliance with France during the Napoleonic Wars. The city surrendered, resulting in the loss of the Danish fleet. The early 19th century saw Denmark transition from an absolute monarchy to a constitutional monarchy.

Industrialization and Modernization (19th Century): The 19th century marked a period of industrialization and urban growth for Copenhagen. Railways were introduced, connecting the city to the rest of Denmark. During this time, Copenhagen's population expanded, and new neighborhoods were established.

The city faced challenges during the Schleswig Wars in the mid-19th century, which ultimately led to the loss of the provinces of Schleswig, Holstein, and Lauenburg to Prussia and Austria.

20th Century and Beyond: Copenhagen navigated through the challenges of two World Wars, during which it was occupied by German forces. After World War II, the city focused on rebuilding and modernizing its infrastructure. Copenhagen's commitment to sustainability, environmental consciousness, and social welfare earned it a reputation as one of the world's most livable cities.

In recent decades, Copenhagen has gained international recognition for its innovative urban planning, bike-friendly infrastructure, and progressive policies. It continues to thrive as a hub for design, architecture, technology, and culture. Landmarks like the Copenhagen Opera House and the modern extension of the Royal Danish Library (known as the Black Diamond) showcase the city's contemporary architectural achievements.

Today, Copenhagen stands as a harmonious blend of its rich historical past and its dynamic present. Its centuries-old landmarks, vibrant neighborhoods, and forward-thinking initiatives make it a captivating destination that embraces both tradition and innovation.

Geography and Climate of Copenhagen

Copenhagen is situated on the eastern coast of the island of Zealand (Sjælland) in Denmark. It is strategically located on the shores of the Øresund Strait, which separates Denmark from Sweden. The city's geographic coordinates are approximately 55.6761° N latitude and 12.5683° E longitude.

The climate of Copenhagen is classified as a temperate maritime climate. Here's a breakdown of the city's climate characteristics:

1 Seasons: Copenhagen experiences distinct four seasons: spring, summer, autumn, and winter.

2 Temperature: Winters (December to February) are relatively mild with average temperatures around 0°C (32°F). Summers (June to August) are comfortably warm, with average temperatures ranging between 17°C to 20°C (63°F to 68°F).

3 Rainfall: Copenhagen receives a moderate amount of rainfall throughout the year, with the wettest months typically being August and October.

4 Sunlight: The city experiences considerable variation in daylight hours throughout the year due to its northern latitude. Summers have long days with extended daylight, while winters have shorter days with limited sunlight.

5. Wind: Being situated near the sea, Copenhagen can experience breezy conditions, especially during the colder months. The sea breeze can have a moderating effect on temperatures.

6. Snowfall: Snow is common during the winter months, and the cityscape can be quite picturesque under a layer of snow.

7. Climate Influences: Copenhagen's climate is influenced by its proximity to the sea, which helps moderate temperatures. The Gulf Stream also plays a role in keeping the winters milder than one might expect at this latitude.

Overall, Copenhagen's climate is relatively mild compared to other northern European cities, making it a comfortable and inviting destination for travelers throughout the year.

People and Culture Of Copenhagen

Copenhagen boasts a vibrant and diverse cultural scene, shaped by its rich history, modern outlook, and Scandinavian roots. Here's a glimpse into the people and culture of this fascinating city:

People:
Copenhagen is home to a diverse population that embraces both its traditional heritage and contemporary global influences. The Danish people are known for their friendly and welcoming nature, often displaying a sense of openness and equality. Many locals are fluent in English, making it easy for visitors to communicate and connect.

Culture:
1 Design and Architecture: Copenhagen is internationally acclaimed for its design and architecture. The city blends historic charm with modern aesthetics, evident in its buildings, public spaces, and interior design. Notable architectural landmarks include the Royal Danish Opera House and the Black Diamond Library.

2. Cuisine: Danish cuisine is a mix of traditional and innovative flavors. Copenhagen is a hub for culinary creativity, with a thriving food scene that ranges from Michelin-starred restaurants to street food markets. Don't miss out on trying Danish pastries ("wienerbrød") and the iconic open-faced sandwiches known as "smørrebrød."

3. Hygge:This unique Danish concept is all about embracing coziness, comfort, and well-being. Copenhagen's culture is deeply influenced by hygge, and you'll find it in the city's cafes, homes, and lifestyle. It's about creating warm and welcoming atmospheres, especially during the colder months.

4. Art and Museums: Copenhagen is a cultural treasure trove, home to world-class museums like the National Gallery of Denmark (SMK) and the Louisiana Museum of Modern Art. The city also hosts various art galleries, exhibitions, and events that showcase both Danish and international artists.

5. Biking Culture: Copenhagen is one of the most bike-friendly cities in the world. Biking is not only a convenient mode of transportation but also a way of life for many residents. The city's extensive network of bike lanes and bike-sharing programs reflect its commitment to sustainability.

6. Music and Festivals: Copenhagen hosts a range of music festivals, from classical to electronic. The city's music scene is vibrant, with numerous venues catering to different tastes. The annual Copenhagen Jazz Festival and Distortion street party are highlights of the cultural calendar.

7. Tolerance and Social Welfare: Copenhagen is known for its progressive social policies and high quality of life. The city prioritizes sustainability, equality, and well-being. The LGBTQ+ community is also embraced, and Copenhagen's Pride Parade is a lively and inclusive event.

Copenhagen's people and culture embody a blend of history, innovation, and an appreciation for the finer things in life. Whether you're exploring its museums, savoring its culinary delights, or simply strolling along its charming streets, you'll experience a city that's both rooted in tradition and looking towards the future.

Health and Tourism In Copenhagen

Healthcare:
Copenhagen offers a well-developed healthcare system, reflective of Denmark's commitment to public health. The city boasts modern hospitals,

clinics, and medical facilities that provide high-quality care to both residents and visitors. For travelers, it's advisable to have travel insurance that covers medical expenses, as healthcare costs can be high. EU citizens can access emergency medical care using the European Health Insurance Card (EHIC), but comprehensive travel insurance is still recommended.

Tourism:
Copenhagen is a popular destination for tourists, drawing visitors with its rich cultural heritage, stunning architecture, and progressive lifestyle. Here's a closer look at tourism in Copenhagen:

1 Sightseeing: The city offers an array of attractions, from historical landmarks like Rosenborg Castle and Christiansborg Palace to contemporary marvels like the Copenhagen Opera House and the Royal Library (Black Diamond). The Little Mermaid statue is an iconic symbol of the city.

2 Cultural Experiences: Copenhagen's museums, galleries, and theaters provide diverse cultural experiences. The National Gallery of Denmark (SMK) and the Ny Carlsberg Glyptotek showcase impressive art collections, while the Tivoli Gardens offer a blend of amusement park fun and cultural events.

3 Food and Culinary Scene: Copenhagen's culinary scene has gained international acclaim. Restaurants like Noma have put Danish cuisine on the map. Additionally, street food markets like Torvehallerne and Reffen offer a variety of tasty options.

4 Shopping: The city is a shopper's paradise, with everything from high-end boutiques on Strøget, Europe's longest pedestrian shopping street, to local designer stores and vintage shops.

5 Green Spaces: Copenhagen's commitment to sustainability is reflected in its green spaces. Parks like King's Garden (Kongens Have) and the Copenhagen Botanical Garden offer serene spots to relax.

6 Biking and Transportation: Copenhagen is known for its bike-friendly infrastructure, making it easy for tourists to explore the city on two wheels. The efficient public transportation system includes buses, trains, and the Metro.

7 Festivals and Events: The city hosts various events and festivals throughout the year, such as the Copenhagen Jazz Festival, Copenhagen Pride, and the Christmas markets.

8 Waterfront Activities: The city's location by the water offers opportunities for harbor tours, canal cruises, and waterfront dining.

9 Day Trips: Copenhagen serves as a gateway to other interesting destinations in Denmark. Easily accessible day trips include visits to Kronborg Castle in Helsingør, the Louisiana Museum of Modern Art in Humlebæk, and the charming town of Roskilde.

Chapter 2: What You Should know Before Heading To Copenhagen

Pre-Travel Tips

Currency: The official currency is the Danish Krone (DKK). Credit cards are widely accepted, but it's a good idea to have some local currency for small purchases.

Language: Danish is the official language, but most Danes speak English fluently. Learning a few basic Danish phrases can be appreciated by locals.

Weather and Clothing: Copenhagen's weather can be changeable, so pack layers and be prepared for rain. Comfortable walking shoes, a waterproof jacket, and an umbrella are recommended.

Transport: Copenhagen has an efficient public transportation system, including buses, trains, and the metro. Consider purchasing a Copenhagen Card for unlimited travel on public transport and free admission to many attractions.

Biking: Copenhagen is incredibly bike-friendly. Renting a bike is a popular and enjoyable way to explore the city.

Tipping: Tipping is not mandatory, as a service charge is usually included in bills. However, rounding up the bill or leaving a small tip is appreciated.

Safety: Copenhagen is generally safe, but be cautious in crowded areas against petty theft. Keep an eye on your belongings.

Opening Hours: Many shops close early on Saturdays and are closed on Sundays. Museums often have a weekly day off, usually Mondays.

Eating Out: Look for the word "smørrebrød" for traditional open-faced sandwiches. Explore the culinary scene with an open mind, as Danish cuisine can be innovative and unique.

Tap Water: Tap water is safe to drink in Copenhagen and is of high quality.

Hygge: Embrace the Danish concept of hygge, which is all about coziness, relaxation, and enjoying life's simple pleasures.

Museums and Attractions: Some attractions may require advance booking or have limited entry. It's a good idea to check opening hours and buy tickets in advance if possible.

Copenhagen Card: Consider purchasing a Copenhagen Card for access to public transport and free entry to many attractions. It can save you money if you plan on visiting multiple sites.

Cultural Etiquette: Danes value personal space and privacy. Be respectful, avoid loud conversations in public spaces, and adhere to local customs.

Electricity: The standard voltage is 230 V, and the standard frequency is 50 Hz. The power plugs are of Type K, which has two round pins and a grounding pin. Danish power outlets use the Europlug (Type C) or Schuko (Type F) plug types, even type E.

Wi-Fi: Most hotels, cafes, and restaurants offer free Wi-Fi. You can also find public Wi-Fi in many areas of the city.

Emergency Numbers: In case of emergency, dial 112 for police, ambulance, or fire services.

Time Zone: Copenhagen operates on Central European Time (CET) during standard time and Central European Summer Time (CEST) during daylight saving time.

Safety: Copenhagen is generally safe, but standard safety precautions apply. Be mindful of your belongings, especially in crowded places and tourist areas.

Drinking Laws: The legal drinking age for alcohol in Denmark is 16 for beer and wine, and 18 for spirits. You can purchase alcohol in supermarkets and special stores ("Vinmonopolet").

Closures: Some attractions, especially museums, may be closed on certain days of the week. Check their websites or information in advance.

Parks and Green Spaces: Copenhagen is known for its parks and green areas. Feel free to enjoy picnics, outdoor activities, and relaxation in these spaces.

Tipping: Tipping is not obligatory in Denmark, as service charges are typically included in bills. However, rounding up the bill or leaving a small tip is appreciated.

By familiarizing yourself with these tips, you'll be well-prepared to make the most of your trip to Copenhagen and fully enjoy all that this wonderful city has to offer.

Best Booking Sites To/ In Copenhagen

Flights:
1. Skyscanner: Allows you to compare flight prices from various airlines and travel agencies to find the best deals.

2. Google Flights: Offers a user-friendly interface to search for flights, compare prices, and track changes in fares.

3. Kayak: Helps you search and compare flights, as well as offers a feature to set up price alerts for your desired routes. (www.kayak.com)

Accommodation:

1 Booking.com: Offers a wide range of hotels, hostels, apartments, and other accommodation options in Copenhagen.(www.booking.com)

2. Expedia: Allows you to book hotels, flights, and car rentals, often offering package deals.(www.expedia.com)

3. Hotels.com: Specializes in hotel bookings and offers a loyalty program for repeat customers. (www.hotels.com)

4. Airbnb: Provides options for booking unique accommodations, such as apartments, homes, and even boats, directly from hosts (www.airbnb.com)

5 TripAdvisor: TripAdvisor provides user-generated reviews, ratings, and recommendations for not just accommodations, attractions . (www.tripadvisor.com)

Transportation:
1. GoEuro (Omio): Helps you compare and book trains, buses, and flights for travel within Europe.

2. Rome2rio: Offers comprehensive information on various transportation options and helps you plan routes between different destinations.

Tours and Activities:
1. Viator: Provides a wide range of tours, activities, and attractions in Copenhagen, allowing you to book experiences in advance.

2. GetYourGuide: Offers a variety of guided tours, attractions, and activities to enhance your Copenhagen experience.

3. Copenhagen Card Official Site: Directly purchase the Copenhagen Card for unlimited public transport and free admission to various attractions.

Travel Insurance:
1. World Nomads: Offers travel insurance that covers medical emergencies, trip cancellations, and more.

2. Allianz Global Assistance: Provides various travel insurance options to suit your needs and trip duration.

Car Rentals:
Rentalcars.com: Offers a wide selection of rental cars from various providers, allowing you to compare prices and choose the best option for your needs.

Cruise Bookings:
CruiseDirect: Allows you to browse and book cruises departing from Copenhagen to various destinations.

Before booking, make sure to read reviews, compare prices, and check for any additional fees or terms and conditions. Using a combination of these booking sites can help you find the best deals and options for your trip to Copenhagen.

Packing Ideas and How To Dress Like Locals In Copenhagen

Clothing:
- Weather-appropriate clothing for the season of your visit (layers are recommended)

- Comfortable walking shoes for exploring the city
- Waterproof shoes or boots for rainy days
- Umbrella and a lightweight, waterproof jacket
- Sweaters or warm layers for cooler evenings
- Casual outfits for daytime sightseeing
- Dressier attire if you plan to visit upscale restaurants or theaters
- Swimwear if you plan to visit during the summer months

Accessories:
- Scarves, gloves, and a hat for colder months
- Sunglasses and sunscreen for sunny days
- Backpack or day bag for carrying essentials during your explorations
- Power bank and travel adapter for charging devices

Travel Essentials:
-Passport, ID, and any necessary travel documents
-Travel insurance information and emergency contact numbers
- Local currency or credit/debit cards and necessary travel cards

- Printed copies of reservations (hotels, flights, tours)
-Printed map of Copenhagen or a reliable navigation app
- Prescription medications and a small first aid kit

Electronics:
- Smartphone and charger
-Camera or smartphone for capturing memories
-Portable charger for keeping your devices powered on-the-go
- Travel adapter if needed for European outlets

Toiletries and Personal Items:
-Toiletries (shampoo, conditioner, soap, toothbrush, toothpaste, etc.)
- Personal hygiene items
- Makeup and skincare products
- Hairbrush or comb
- Menstrual products if needed
- Any special medications or personal health items

Miscellaneous:
- Reusable water bottle
- Snacks for on-the-go (granola bars, nuts, etc.)
- Travel pillow and eye mask for comfortable sleep on flights or trains
- Guidebook or maps of Copenhagen
- Local SIM card or international data plan for staying connected
- Language Guide: Although many people speak English, having a basic Danish phrasebook can be helpful of app like Duolingo.

Note: Copenhagen is known for its casual and stylish fashion sense. Packing clothes that can be easily layered will help you adapt to the changing weather and fit in with the local style. Don't forget to also pack a sense of adventure and curiosity to make the most of your trip to this vibrant city!

How To Dress Like Locals In Copenhagen

Dressing like a local in Copenhagen means embracing a stylish yet functional and comfortable approach to fashion inorder to blend with the locals as tourists. The city's residents often exhibit a chic and minimalist style that combines classic pieces with contemporary elements. Here's a comprehensive guide to dressing like a local in Copenhagen:

Neutral Color Palette:
Opt for a neutral color palette with shades like black, white, gray, navy, and beige. These colors are versatile and easy to mix and match.

Minimalist Silhouettes:
Choose clean and minimalist silhouettes. Stick to well-fitted clothing that isn't overly flashy or complicated.

High-Quality Basics:
Invest in high-quality basics like well-fitting jeans, tailored trousers, and classic white shirts. These pieces form the foundation of a Copenhagen wardrobe.

Layering:
Layering is essential in Copenhagen due to the changing weather. Pair a basic T-shirt with a lightweight sweater or cardigan, and add a stylish jacket or coat on top.

Functional Outerwear:
Invest in a stylish yet functional coat or jacket for colder months. Trench coats, wool coats, and leather jackets are popular choices.

Comfortable Footwear:
Copenhagen is a walking and biking city, so comfortable footwear is key. Opt for stylish sneakers, ankle boots, or well-made flats that you can walk in for hours.

Quality Accessories:
Choose quality over quantity when it comes to accessories. A well-made leather bag, a timeless watch, and understated jewelry can elevate your look.

Sustainable Fashion:
Copenhagen values sustainability, so consider incorporating sustainable fashion choices into your wardrobe. Look for eco-friendly fabrics, ethical brands, and secondhand pieces.

Embrace Hygge:
Hygge is a Danish concept that emphasizes coziness and comfort. Incorporate soft and cozy materials like knitwear, scarves, and oversized sweaters into your outfits.

Bold Accessories:
While the overall style is often minimalist, Copenhageners often add a touch of personality through bold accessories like statement earrings, scarves, or hats.

Casual Elegance:
Copenhageners excel at achieving a casual yet elegant look. A pair of well-fitted jeans or trousers paired with a simple blouse and elegant shoes can strike this balance.

All-Weather Attire:
Be prepared for all types of weather. Bring an umbrella, a rainproof jacket, and a scarf or hat for warmth.

Don't Overdo It:
Copenhageners tend to avoid flashy, overly trendy items. Instead, focus on well-tailored, understated pieces that exude confidence.

Remember, the key to dressing like a local in Copenhagen is to prioritize comfort, quality, and timeless style. Embrace a minimalist approach and focus on pieces that can be mixed and matched easily. Pay attention to the weather and adapt your clothing choices accordingly.

Copenhagen Weather

Copenhagen experiences a temperate maritime climate with four distinct seasons. Here's a comprehensive overview of the weather you can expect in each season:

Spring (March to May):

Average High Temperatures: 5°C to 13°C (41°F to 55°F)

Average Low Temperatures: 0°C to 6°C (32°F to 43°F)

Weather: Spring in Copenhagen starts off cool and gradually warms up. March can still be chilly, but by May, temperatures become milder.

Precipitation: Moderate rainfall, occasional sunny days.

What to Pack: Light layers, sweaters, a rainproof jacket, and comfortable shoes for walking.

Summer (June to August):

Average High Temperatures: 20°C to 23°C (68°F to 73°F)

Average Low Temperatures: 12°C to 15°C (54°F to 59°F)

Weather: Summer is the warmest season in Copenhagen. Days are pleasant and nights are relatively cool.

Precipitation: Generally dry with occasional showers.

What to Pack: T-shirts, shorts, dresses, sunglasses, sunscreen, a light jacket for cooler evenings.

Autumn (September to November):

Average High Temperatures: 16°C to 9°C (61°F to 48°F)
Average Low Temperatures: 9°C to 2°C (48°F to 36°F)
Weather: Autumn sees a gradual cooling down and changing foliage. September is still mild, while November becomes colder.
Precipitation: Increasing rainfall and occasional windy days.
What to Pack: Sweaters, long-sleeve shirts, jackets, scarves, and waterproof footwear.

Winter (December to February):

Average High Temperatures: 2°C to 3°C (36°F to 37°F)
Average Low Temperatures: -1°C to -2°C (30°F to 28°F)

Weather: Winters in Copenhagen are cold with occasional snowfall. December and January are the coldest months.

Precipitation: Some snowfall, chilly and damp conditions.

What to Pack: Warm layers, insulated coat, gloves, hat, scarf, sturdy winter boots.

Keep in mind that weather can vary from year to year, so it's a good idea to check the forecast closer to your travel dates. Regardless of the season, Copenhagen offers unique experiences and attractions, making it a wonderful destination year-round.

Best Time To Visit Copenhagen

Choosing the best time to travel to Copenhagen depends on your preferences and the type of experience you're seeking. Here's are tips to help you decide:

Spring (March to May):

- **Weather**: Mild temperatures, occasional rain, and blooming flowers.
- **Pros**: Fewer tourists, longer daylight hours, and a vibrant atmosphere.
- **Cons**: Unpredictable weather and cooler temperatures in March.
- **Best for**: Exploring outdoor attractions, enjoying cultural events, and experiencing the city's blossoming gardens.

Summer (June to August):

- **Weather**: Warm and pleasant temperatures, longer days.
- **Pros**: Lively atmosphere, outdoor festivals, and beach activities.
- **Cons**: Peak tourist season, higher prices, and more crowded attractions.
- **Best for:** Enjoying parks, beaches, boat tours, and experiencing the city's vibrant outdoor culture.

Autumn (September to November):

- **Weather**: Mild temperatures, beautiful fall foliage, occasional rain.
- **Pros**: Fewer tourists, cozy atmosphere, and cultural events.
- **Cons**: Increasing rainfall and shorter days.
- **Best for**: Exploring museums, art galleries, experiencing the city's cafes and restaurants, and enjoying the colorful streets.

Winter (December to February):

- **Weather**: Cold temperatures, occasional snowfall.
- **Pros**: Fewer tourists, festive holiday markets, and a cozy hygge atmosphere.
- **Cons**: Short days, limited daylight, and colder weather.
- **Best for:** Visiting Christmas markets, enjoying indoor attractions, savoring Danish comfort food, and experiencing the unique charm of winter in Copenhagen.

Things To Consider When Choosing Best Time To Visit Copenhagen;

- **Budget**: Summer is the peak tourist season, so prices for accommodations and flights are often higher. Spring and autumn offer a good balance of pleasant weather and fewer crowds.

-**Weather Preferences**: If you prefer warmer weather and longer daylight hours, opt for spring and summer. If you enjoy a cozy winter atmosphere and holiday festivities, winter might be your choice.

-**Activities**: Different seasons offer unique activities. Outdoor enthusiasts will love summer, while those interested in cultural events might prefer spring or autumn.

-**Cultural Events:** Copenhagen hosts various events and festivals throughout the year, such as the Copenhagen Jazz Festival in July and Christmas markets in December.

-**Daylight** Hours: Keep in mind that daylight hours are shorter in winter, which can impact the amount of sightseeing you can do in a day.

-**Peak Season**: Summer is the peak tourist season with the warmest weather and longer days. Book accommodations well in advance if traveling during this time.

-**Shoulder Seasons:** Spring and autumn offer pleasant weather, fewer crowds, and cultural events. Prices for accommodation and attractions may be more reasonable compared to summer.

-**Off-Season**: Winter is the least crowded time to visit, making it ideal for budget travelers and those who enjoy a cozy atmosphere.

Ultimately, the best time to travel to Copenhagen depends on your interests and what you want to experience during your trip. Copenhagen's charm is ever-present, and each season brings its own special allure to the city.

Visa Requirements To Copenhagen, Denmark

What kind of visa is required for entry into Copenhagen, Denmark?

The procedure for applying for a visa to Copenhagen, Denmark depends on why you want to go there. The kind of Danish visa you need for short-stay visits should be determined before you begin the application procedure.

You may apply for one of the following Schengen visa categories for Denmark depending on your reason for entry and stay:

1 Danish Airport Transit Permit. enables you to arrive at a Danish airport and then board a flight to a non-Schengen nation.

2 **Danish Transit Permit**. primarily for sailors who must embark in a Danish port to board another ship to go to or from a non-Schengen country

3 Tourist or visitor visa for Denmark. enables you to go to Denmark for vacation, exploration, sightseeing, or to meet friends and relatives.

4 Denmark Business Permit. It permits you to visit the country to take part in business meetings or other relevant activities.

5 **A Danish visa is required for an official visit**. If you are a member of a foreign official delegation invited to Denmark for an official visit, apply for this visa.

6 **Medical Visa for Denmark**. the visa required for entering Denmark for medical treatment.

7 **Denmark study permit**. With this sort of visa, you can enroll in a three-month study program at a Danish educational institution.

8 **Visa for Denmark for film, sports, and cultural crews**. To attend a sporting or cultural event in Denmark, apply to enter the Schengen area.

Visa Requirements for a Schengen Visa Application for Copenhagen, Denmark?

Tips; Use your computer to fill out the form, print it, and then sign it at the bottom.

The following are the mandatory Danish visa requirements:

-**Two photographs for a passport.** For applications for Danish Schengen visas, the images must match and adhere to the photograph specifications.

-**Your current passport**. As previously said, verify that your passport has:

- Two blank papers are needed to attach the visa.

- Not more than ten years old,
- Has a validity of at least three months beyond the day you want to depart Denmark and the whole Schengen region

-**Copies of any prior visas you may have had.**

-**Travel health insurance for Denmark**. Evidence proving you have travel health insurance that pays out at least 30,000 euros for any medical emergency and covers the whole Schengen region, including Denmark.

-**Route of a round-trip flight**. a flight booking confirmation for entering and leaving Denmark. The names, dates, and flight numbers should all be included in this paper.

-**Evidence of accommodations**. Evidence, such as a hotel reservation, that demonstrates where you will be staying during your visit to Denmark.

-**Proof of citizenship.** This might be a marriage license, a child's birth certificate, a spouse's death certificate, etc.

-**Evidence of enough financial resources for the duration of the stay in Denmark**. If staying in a hotel, you must be able to vouch for having around 67.24€ every day you intend to spend in Denmark, whereas if staying in a hostel or other less expensive kind of lodging, you must have approximately 47.07€.

-**A covering letter**. a private letter outlining your reasons for wanting to visit Denmark, your plans for the trip's duration, your departure date, and other pertinent information.

Additional Visa Requirements for Denmark Depending on Your Employment status

Depending on your employment situation, you may need to meet the following extra conditions for a Danish visa:

If employed:

- Employment contract
- The most recent six months bank statements
- Employer Income
- Tax Return (ITR) form or leave authorization

If self-employed:

- Copy of your company license
- Income Tax Return (ITR) of the company
- Bank account for the previous six months

If a student:

- Evidence of enrolment
- A letter of approval from a school or institution
- Advertisements

If retired:

- The most recent six-month pension statement

If applicable

- Proof of consistent property income for the last six months

Additional Danish Minor Visa Requirements

Parents requesting a short-stay visa for a minor child or a minor themselves must fulfill the following additional Danish visa requirements in their application file:

- Birth document for the young person visiting Denmark.

- The parents' signatures are on the application for Denmark.
- Family court order. Under circumstances when a kid has exclusive custody of one parent.
- Certified copies of both parents' IDs or passports.
- If the minor is traveling alone, a notarized parental authorization to visit Denmark is signed by both parents or guardians.

Where Can I Apply for a Short-Stay Danish Visa?

Each nation where Denmark has a presence has its visa requirements. You may thus have to apply to one of the following Denmark diplomatic missions in your home country:

- The Embassy of Denmark
- A Danish consulate
- A Visa Application Center where Denmark has contracted out the filing of visas

- The Embassy or Consulate of another Schengen nation that Denmark has contracted with for the filing of visas

How long can we remain without a visa in Denmark?

Whether you can enter Denmark at all or for how long you can stay without a visa depends on your nationality.

Within 180 days, nationals of EU/EEA members are permitted to remain in Denmark for up to 90 days. They must register with the appropriate Danish authorities if they want to stay longer.

Passport holders from nations without visa requirements for Denmark are permitted up to 90 days of stay in Denmark and the other Schengen nations every six months.

- Australian, Israeli, Japanese, Canadian, New Zealand, South Korean, and American nationals who desire to remain longer in Denmark must apply for a residence visa with the appropriate Danish authorities within three months of their arrival.

- If citizens of the remaining visa-exempt nations want to stay longer in Denmark, they must apply for a Denmark National visa for long stays from their home country.

Nationals of those nations who have not yet ratified a visa-free travel pact with Denmark are required to get a visa before entering Denmark or any other Schengen member country,

Can I Extend My Denmark Schengen visa?

Yes, you may extend your Danish Schengen visa, but only in extraordinary circumstances when new information and unique circumstances develop after you enter Denmark, such as force majeure or humanitarian considerations. The Danish Immigration Service and, under certain circumstances, the Danish Police are the entities in charge of extending visas in Denmark.

Copenhagen Useful Phrases

Some useful and surviving phrases for your trip to Copenhagen:

1. **Greetings:**
   - Hello: Hej
   - Good morning: Godmorgen
   - Good afternoon: God eftermiddag
   - Good evening: Godaften
   - How are you?: Hvordan har du det?

2. **Basic Conversations**:
   - What's your name?: Hvad hedder du?
   - My name is...: Jeg hedder...
   - Yes: Ja
   - No: Nej
   - Please: Vær så venlig
   - Thank you: Tak
   - Excuse me: Undskyld mig
   - Sorry: Undskyld
   - I don't understand: Jeg forstår ikke

-Bathroom: Toilet / Badeværelse

-I'm lost: Jeg har mistet mig

-Help!: Hjælp!

-What time is it?: Hvad er klokken?

-I'm a tourist: Jeg er turist

-Is there an English menu?: Er der en engelsk menu?

-I need medical help: Jeg har brug for lægehjælp

-Could you take a photo of me, please?: Vil du tage et billede af mig, tak?

-Call the police: Ring til politiet

-Where is the nearest hospital?: Hvor er det nærmeste hospital?

3. **Getting Around:**

- Where is...?: Hvor er...?

- How much is this?: Hvor meget koster det?

- I would like to go to...: Jeg vil gerne tage til...

- Can you help me?: Kan du hjælpe mig?

- Bus station: Busstation

- Train station: Togstation

- Metro: Metro

-Bus stop - Busstoppested

-Airport - Lufthavn

-Where can I find a taxi?: Hvor kan jeg finde en taxa?

-Where's the nearest metro station?: Hvor er den nærmeste metrostation?

4. **Dining**:

-Food: Mad

- I would like...: Jeg vil gerne have...

- Menu, please: Menukort, tak

- Water: Vand

- Coffee: Kaffe

- Bill, please: Regningen, tak

- Delicious: Lækkert

- Cheers!: Skål!

-I'm vegetarian / vegan - Jeg er vegetar / veganer (Yay air veh-geh-tar / veh-gah-ner)

-Table for [number] please - Et bord til [number], tak (Eht boor til [number], tahk)

-Can you recommend a good restaurant? - Kan du anbefale en god restaurant?

-What are the must-see attractions? - Hvad er de mest seværdige attraktioner?

-Can you suggest a local experience? - Kan du foreslå en lokal oplevelse?

-Where is the restroom? - Hvor er toilettet? (Vor air toy-let?)

- Morgenmad (morn mell): Breakfast

- Mellemmåltid (mellem maltwo): Snack

- Frokost (fro kust): Lunch

-Eftermiddagste (efter mid-e ste): Afternoon tea

-Middag (mee da): Dinner

-Dessert (de-sssert): Dessert

5. Directions:

— Left - Venstre (Ven-streh)

— Right - Højre (Hoy-reh)

— Straight ahead - Lige ud (Lee-yeh ooth)

— Øst (ust): East

— Vest (west): West

— Nord (no-ah): North

— Syd (sue): South

— Udenfor/idenfor: Outside/inside

— Overfor: Opposite

— Mod: Toward

6. **Shopping**:

- How much does this cost?: Hvor meget koster det?

- Can I try this on?: Kan jeg prøve det her?

- Do you have it in a different color/size?: Har du det i en anden farve/størrelse?

- I'll take it: Jeg tager den/det

-Do you accept credit cards? - Tager I imod kreditkort?

7. **Cultural Etiquette:**

-Please speak slowly: Vil du tale langsomt, tak?

-Is it okay to take photos here?: Er det ok at tage billeder her?

-May I enter?: Må jeg komme ind?

-Thank you for your hospitality: Tak for jeres gæstfrihed

Remember to be polite and use these phrases to show your respect for the local culture. Enjoy your time in Copenhagen!

Tips; *To learn language, make use of these*

- Babbel
- Google Translate
- Duolingo

Chapter 3: Getting To And Around Copenhagen

Getting To Copenhagen

By Air

Copenhagen Airport (Kastrup Airport) is the primary international gateway to the city. It's well-connected to major cities worldwide. Here's how to get there:

1. **From Europe:** Numerous airlines offer direct flights to Copenhagen from major European cities. Look for flights on airlines like SAS, Norwegian, Lufthansa, British Airways, and more.

2. **From North America**: Many major North American cities offer flights to Copenhagen with one or more layovers. Airlines such as Delta, United, Air Canada, and SAS operate these routes.

3. **From Asia:** Flights from Asian cities usually involve one or more layovers. Airlines like Qatar Airways, Emirates, and Turkish Airlines provide options.

4 **Domestic Flights**: If you're traveling within Denmark, there are domestic flights connecting Copenhagen to other Danish cities.

Check flight search engines like Skyscanner, Google Flights, or Kayak to compare options.

By Train:
Copenhagen has a well-connected rail network that links it to various European cities;

1 From Other European Cities: The EuroCity (EC) and InterCity (IC) trains connect Copenhagen to cities like Hamburg, Berlin, and Stockholm. You can also take the high-speed Öresundståg train across the Öresund Bridge to Malmö in Sweden.

2 Within Denmark: The Danish railway system connects Copenhagen to cities like Aarhus, Odense, and Aalborg.

By Bus:
Long-distance buses operated by companies like FlixBus connect Copenhagen to neighboring cities and countries. Buses are generally a more economical option for travel within Europe.

1 **International Buses**: Several bus companies operate routes to Copenhagen from cities like Hamburg, Berlin, and Oslo.

2 **Within Denmark**: Domestic buses connect Copenhagen to various cities within Denmark.

By Ferry:

If you're coming from Sweden, you can take a ferry from cities like Malmö to Copenhagen. The ferry ride offers beautiful views of the Øresund Strait. The ferry terminal is located in the northern part of Copenhagen

By Car:

If you're planning to drive to Copenhagen, you can use the well-maintained road networks connecting Denmark to neighboring countries. Remember to check for road regulations, tolls, and parking options.

Popular routes to Copenhagen

Stockholm to Copenhagen

Berlin to Copenhagen

Hamburg to Copenhagen

Amsterdam to Copenhagen

Gothenburg to Copenhagen

Malmö to Copenhagen

Paris to Copenhagen

Oslo to Copenhagen

Brussels to Copenhagen

London to Copenhagen

Useful Tips:

-Consider using travel apps to check flight, train, and bus schedules, as well as public transportation routes and real-time updates.

-Check visa requirements and travel restrictions before your trip, as they may vary based on your nationality and the current global situation.

-It's a good idea to have some local currency (Danish Krone) on hand for small purchases, although credit cards are widely accepted.

Getting Around Copenhagen

- **Public Transport:**

Copenhagen has an efficient and well-integrated public transportation system that includes buses, trains, and the metro. Here's how to navigate the public transport system:

1. **Metro**: The Copenhagen Metro (Metroen) is a fast and convenient way to travel within the city. It consists of two lines, M1 and M2, which

connect key areas, including the city center, the airport, and various neighborhoods.

2. **Buses**: Buses cover a wide network and connect areas not directly accessible by the metro. They are a good option for reaching destinations not served by the metro lines.

3. **Trains**: The S-train network connects the city with its suburbs. The trains are well-connected and efficient, making them a useful option for traveling to areas outside the city center.

City Passes:
Consider purchasing a City Pass, which provides unlimited travel on public transport (buses, trains, metro), as well as discounts on admission to various attractions. There are different types of City Passes available for different durations.

Biking:
Copenhagen is renowned for its bike-friendly infrastructure, and biking is a popular way to get around. You can rent bikes from various bike rental shops or use the city's bike-sharing

program. Be sure to follow local biking rules and use hand signals when cycling.

Walking:
Many of Copenhagen's attractions are within walking distance of each other, especially in the city center. Exploring on foot allows you to fully immerse yourself in the city's charm and discover hidden gems.

Taxis and Ride-Sharing:
Taxis are readily available in Copenhagen, but they are relatively expensive compared to public transport. Ride-sharing services like Uber are also operational in the city. Examples of taxi in Copenhagen are;

Dantaxi 4x48
TAXA 4x35
Taxi 4x27

Ferries:
Copenhagen has a network of ferries that provide an alternative way to travel across the city's waterways. The ferry system connects various neighborhoods and offers scenic views.

Car Rental:

While public transportation is efficient, you might choose to rent a car if you plan to explore areas outside Copenhagen. However, keep in mind that parking in the city can be both limited and costly. Examples of car rentals in Copenhagen are;

Avis
Sixt Rent a Car
Europcar
Hertz

Hop-On Hop-Off Buses and Boats:

These tourist-friendly services provide guided tours with the flexibility to get on and off at various attractions. They offer a convenient way to see the city's highlights while learning about its history and culture.

Boat;

Copenhagen may also be explored by boat. Canal tours give guided tours of the port and canals that last an hour and leave from locations including Nyhavn and Gammel Strand. Depending on the operator, prices (in Danish kroner or euros) range from $4 to $6.50 for children to $10 to $13 for adults. For 99 kroner (about $16) per adult, Stromma Denmark also offers hop-on, hop-off services along one of the numerous canals. On the website of Wonderful Copenhagen, you may find a list of boat excursion providers such as;

Stromma Denmark
Netto-Badene

Tips!

- **Copenhagen Card:**
  Consider getting the Copenhagen Card, which provides free unlimited travel on public transport, including trains, buses, and the metro. It also offers free entry or discounts to numerous attractions, making it a cost-effective option for exploring the city.

- **Tickets**:
  You can purchase tickets for public transport at metro stations, train stations, and online. Consider using the Rejsekort,

a smart card that offers convenient fare payment for all types of public transport.

- **Travel Apps:**
  Download the official transportation apps for Copenhagen, such as "Rejseplanen" for planning routes and checking schedules, and "DOT Mobilbilletter" for purchasing mobile tickets for public transport.

- Be mindful of bike lanes and pedestrian crossings while walking or biking.

- Copenhagen is known for its green initiatives, so be sure to follow recycling and waste disposal guidelines.

Chapter 4: Where To Stay In Copenhagen

Copenhagen is a vibrant city with various neighborhoods, each offering a unique atmosphere. Here's a brief overview of some popular areas to stay in:

1. **Indre By (City Center):** This area is ideal for first-time visitors, as it's close to major attractions like Tivoli Gardens, Nyhavn, and the Round Tower. Expect a mix of historic architecture, shopping, and dining options.

2. **Vesterbro**: Known for its hipster vibe, Vesterbro has trendy boutiques, art galleries, and a lively nightlife. The Meatpacking District is a highlight, featuring numerous restaurants and bars.

3. **Nørrebro**: A multicultural neighborhood with a youthful energy. You'll find a blend of cafes, vintage shops, and green spaces like Assistens Cemetery. It's a great spot for a diverse dining scene.

4. **Østerbro**: A family-friendly area with leafy streets and parks, including Fælledparken. It's quieter than some other neighborhoods but offers a relaxed atmosphere.

5. **Frederiksberg**: A more upscale district with beautiful gardens and Frederiksberg Palace. The area has a mix of shopping, dining, and cultural attractions.

6. **Christianshavn**: Known for its canals and charming waterfront buildings, this area offers a laid-back atmosphere. The famous Freetown Christiania is also located here.

7. **Amager**: Close to the airport and the beach, Amager is becoming increasingly popular. It offers a mix of residential areas, parks, and cultural attractions.

8. **Kødbyen (Meatpacking District)**: Located in Vesterbro, it's a dynamic area with trendy restaurants, bars, and creative spaces.

9. **Hellerup**: A posh and upscale suburb known for its waterfront properties and upscale boutiques.

10. **Kongens Nytorv**: A central square with easy access to attractions and transportation, making it a convenient base for exploring the city.

11.Osterport Station Area: A convenient location for transport connections, with easy access to the Little Mermaid statue and Kastellet fortress.

12. **Vesterport**: Close to the central station, this area is convenient for travelers and offers a mix of hotels, restaurants, and shops.

Best Hotels To Stay In Copenhagen

Copenhagen offers a wide range of hotels to suit various preferences and budgets. Here's a list of some of the best hotels in the city:

Hotel D'Angleterre:

A luxury 5-star hotel located in the heart of the city. Known for its elegant décor, impeccable service, and stunning views of Kongens Nytorv Square.

Nimb Hotel:

Situated in Tivoli Gardens, this boutique hotel exudes charm and opulence. Guests can enjoy direct access to the amusement park and exquisite dining options.

Hotel Nørreport:

A modern and stylish option located near Nørreport Station. It's known for its contemporary design, central location, and comfortable rooms.

Copenhagen Marriott Hotel:

Overlooking the waterfront, this hotel offers spacious rooms, a fitness center, and fantastic views of the city. It's conveniently located near popular attractions.

Hotel SP34:

A trendy boutique hotel in the Latin Quarter, known for its Scandinavian design, vibrant atmosphere, and proximity to cafes and shops.

Ibsens Hotel:

Located in Nørrebro, this cozy and eclectic hotel features individually decorated rooms, a charming courtyard, and a relaxed ambiance.

Hotel Alexandra:

This mid-century modern hotel is known for its unique retro design and central location near Tivoli Gardens and the Central Station.

71 Nyhavn Hotel:

Situated in the historic Nyhavn Harbor, this hotel offers waterfront views, stylish rooms, and a location close to many attractions.

Andersen Boutique Hotel:

Located in Vesterbro, this boutique hotel features colorful and modern design, eco-friendly amenities, and a cozy atmosphere.

Sanders Hotel:

A boutique hotel in the heart of Copenhagen, known for its Scandinavian design, rooftop terrace, and cozy atmosphere.

Copenhagen Admiral Hotel:

Housed in a historic warehouse, this waterfront hotel offers unique rooms and a central location near Amalienborg Palace.

Nobis Hotel Copenhagen:

A contemporary luxury hotel in a prime central location, offering stylish rooms, a spa, and a chic restaurant.

Urban House Copenhagen:

A budget-friendly option with a youthful and vibrant atmosphere, offering both private and shared rooms.

Copenhagen Downtown Hostel:

Centrally located hostel with clean and modern accommodations, perfect for budget travelers.

CABINN City Hotel:

A no-frills hotel with compact rooms, offering a convenient location close to Tivoli Gardens and the central station.

Kids Friendly Hotels In Copenhagen

Tivoli Hotel & Congress Center:

This hotel is directly connected to Tivoli Gardens and offers family-friendly rooms, a playroom, and a swimming pool with a waterslide.

Copenhagen Strand Hotel:

Situated by the waterfront, this hotel provides family rooms and is within walking distance of Nyhavn and other attractions.

Copenhagen Island Hotel:

With a modern design, this hotel offers family rooms and features a kids' corner in the lobby.

Absalon Hotel:

This boutique hotel offers family rooms and is located near the central station, making it convenient for exploring the city.

Hotel Kong Arthur:

This family-friendly hotel offers a cozy atmosphere and features a playroom, board games, and a relaxing inner courtyard.

Hotel Skt. Petri:

Located in the Latin Quarter, this stylish hotel offers family rooms and is close to many cultural attractions.

Pets Friendly Hotels In Copenhagen

Scandic Copenhagen: This hotel is known for its pet-friendly policies and offers comfortable accommodations for both you and your pet.

Copenhagen Island Hotel: With a waterfront location, this hotel is pet-friendly and provides a welcoming atmosphere for both guests and their pets.

Adina Apartment Hotel Copenhagen: Offering apartment-style accommodations, this hotel is pet-friendly and suitable for travelers who want more space for their pets.

Axel Guldsmeden: This eco-friendly boutique hotel welcomes pets and provides a charming and relaxed environment.

Urban House Copenhagen by MEININGER: This budget-friendly hotel allows pets and has a playful design that's accommodating for both guests and their furry friends.

Wakeup Copenhagen: With various locations in the city, this budget hotel chain allows pets and provides affordable accommodations.

Radisson Blu Scandinavia Hotel: This hotel is known for being pet-friendly and offers convenient access to Tivoli Gardens and other attractions

Chapter 5; Top Tourist Attractions In Copenhagen

Copenhagen is filled with numerous tourist attractions that offer a blend of history, culture, and modernity. Here's a guide to some of the top attractions you shouldn't miss:

Tivoli Gardens:

A historic amusement park and garden with rides, games, concerts, and beautiful scenery. It's especially magical during the holiday season.

The Little Mermaid:

This iconic statue by the water is based on Hans Christian Andersen's fairy tale and is one of Copenhagen's most recognizable symbols.

Nyhavn:

A picturesque waterfront district with colorful buildings, boats, and a vibrant atmosphere. It's a great place to stroll, dine, and enjoy the view.

The Round Tower (Rundetaarn):

A unique 17th-century tower with a spiral ramp instead of stairs, offering panoramic views of the city.

Amalienborg Palace:

The official residence of the Danish royal family, consisting of four identical palace buildings surrounding a central square.

Rosenborg Castle:

A well-preserved Renaissance castle housing the Danish Crown Jewels and featuring beautiful gardens.

Christiansborg Palace:

Home to the Danish Parliament, Supreme Court, and Prime Minister's Office. Visitors can explore the palace's elegant rooms and tower for panoramic views.

National Museum of Denmark:

A comprehensive museum showcasing Danish history, culture, and artifacts from ancient times to the present.

Design museum Danmark:

This museum focuses on Danish design and decorative arts, featuring furniture, ceramics, fashion, and more.

Louisiana Museum of Modern Art:

Although located just outside Copenhagen, this museum is worth a visit for its impressive collection of contemporary art and stunning coastal setting.

Copenhagen Zoo:

One of the oldest zoos in Europe, offering a diverse range of animals and exhibits in a spacious and well-maintained environment.

Church of Our Saviour (Vor Frelsers Kirke):

Known for its unique spiral staircase that leads to a panoramic viewing platform atop the tower. **Frederiksborg Castle:**

Situated in Hillerød, a short train ride from Copenhagen, this stunning Renaissance castle houses the Museum of National History.

Canal Tours:

Exploring the city's canals by boat provides a unique perspective on Copenhagen's architecture and landmarks.

The Black Diamond (Royal Library):

A modern waterfront building housing the national library and cultural center, offering exhibitions, concerts, and a unique architecture.

The National Gallery of Denmark (Statens Museum for Kunst):

Denmark's largest art museum, featuring an impressive collection of European art from the Renaissance to modern times.

Kids Friendly Tourist Attractions

Copenhagen Zoo: A family-friendly zoo with a diverse collection of animals, including elephants, lions, pandas, and more. The Children's Zoo area offers interactive exhibits.

Experimentarium: An interactive science museum where kids can engage in hands-on experiments, explore different scientific concepts, and have fun learning.

National Aquarium Denmark (Den Blå Planet): The largest aquarium in Northern Europe, offering a mesmerizing underwater experience with diverse marine life.

Copenhagen's Playgrounds: The city is dotted with playgrounds and parks, including the unique Superkilen Park, where kids can enjoy various play areas, sculptures, and skateboarding ramps.

The Worker's Museum: A museum dedicated to the history of work and labor in Denmark, with interactive displays and activities suitable for kids.

Cirkusmuseet (Circus Museum): This museum offers a glimpse into the world of circus with costumes, props, and interactive exhibits.

Planetarium: A space-themed attraction featuring a planetarium dome where kids can learn about stars, planets, and the universe through immersive shows.

Copenhagen's Beaches: During the warmer months, take the kids to Amager Beach Park or Bellevue Beach for some sandcastle building and swimming.

Naturbornholm: If you're up for a day trip, take a ferry to Bornholm Island and visit this interactive nature and science center that's both educational and entertaining.

Copenhagen Airport Playground: If you have some time to spare at the airport, the play area here can help kids burn off energy before or after a flight.

Chapter 6: Best Restaurants In Copenhagen

1 Marv & Ben

Address; Snaregade 4, 1205 København, Denmark

Opens and closes;

Saturday   5:30 pm–1 am
Sunday   5:30 pm–1 am

Monday	5:30 pm–1 am
Tuesday	5:30 pm–1 am
Wednesday	5:30 pm–1 am
Thursday	5:30 pm–1 am
Friday	5:30 pm–1 am

2 Restaurant Karla

Address: Dantes Plads 1, 1556 København V, Denmark

Opens and closes

| Sunday | 11:30 am–11:30 pm |

Monday   11:30 am–11:30 pm
Tuesday   11:30 am–11:30 pm
Wednesday 11:30 am–11:30 pm
Thursday   11:30 am–11:30 pm
Friday.   11:30 am–11:30 pm
Saturday   11:30 am–11:30 pm

3. Maple Casual Dining

Address: Vesterbrogade 24, 1620 København, Denmark

Opens and closes

Saturday	5–9:30 pm
Sunday	5–9 pm
Monday	5–9 pm
Tuesday	5–9 pm
Wednesday	5–9 pm
Thursday	5–9:30 pm
Friday.	5–9:30 pm

4. Schønnemann

Address: Hauser Pl. 16, 1127 København, Denmark

Opens and closes

Saturday 11:30 am–5 pm
Sunday 11:30 am–5 pm
Monday 11:30 am–5 pm
Tuesday 11:30 am–5 pm
Wednesday 11:30 am–5 pm
Thursday 11:30 am–5 pm
Friday 11:30 am–5 pm

5. Krebsegaarden

Address: Studiestræde 17, 1455 København, Denmark

Opens and closes

Sunday   Closed
Monday   Closed
Tuesday   6 pm–12 am
Wednesday   6 pm–12 am
Thursday   6 pm–12 am
Friday   6 pm–12 am
Saturday   6 pm–12 am

6 Restaurant Barr

Address: Strandgade 93, 1401 København, Denmark

Opens and closes

Sunday	Closed
Monday	5–11 pm
Tuesday	5–11 pm
Wednesday	5–11 pm
Thursday	12 pm–12 am
Friday	12 pm–12 am
Saturday	12 pm–12 am

7. The Olive Kitchen & Bar

Address: Nørregade 22, 1165 København, Denmark

Opens and closes

Sunday   5–9 pm
Monday   5–9 pm
Tuesday   5–9 pm
Wednesday 5–9 pm
Thursday   5–9:30 pm
Friday.   5–9:30 pm
Saturday   5–9:30 pm

8 Noma

Address: Refshalevej 96, 1432 København K, Denmark

Opens and closes

Sunday   Closed
Monday   Closed
Tuesday   5–11 pm
Wednesday   5–11 pm
Thursday   5–11 pm
Friday.   12–5 pm
              6–11 pm
Saturday   Closed

9. Kødbyens Fiskebar

Address: Flæsketorvet 100, 1711 København, Denmark

Opens and closes

Sunday	11:30 am–12 am
Monday	11:30 am–12 am
Tuesday	11:30 am–12 am
Wednesday	11:30 am–12 am
Thursday	11:30 am–12 am
Friday.	11:30 am–1 am
Saturday	11:30 am–1 am

10. Bæst

Address: Guldbergsgade 29, 2200 København, Denmark

Opens and closes

Sunday	11 am–2:30 pm
	5–10 pm
Monday	Closed
Tuesday	5–10 pm
Wednesday	5–10 pm
Thursday	5–10 pm
Friday	5–10 pm
Saturday	11 am–2:30 pm
	5–10 pm

Street Food Markets

Do you like to eat somewhere with a wide selection of cuisines and be surrounded by locals? Then, we advise stopping at a street food market to refuel. Street food markets may be found in Denmark's major cities, such as Storms Pakhus in Odense, The Lighthouse Street Food in Aalborg, Aarhus Street Food at the bus station, and Reffen Street Food in Copenhagen.

1 Det Fedtede Hjørne - Street Food

The greatest street food Hornbaek has to offer can be found at "The Greasy Corner," a beachfront market where a variety of foods and hot and cold beverages may be sampled.

Address: Øresundsvej 2A, 3100 Hornbæk

2 Storms Pakhus- a culinary and inventive food market; A brand-new, atmospheric food market with an international layout has opened in Storms Pakhus' unfinished industrial warehouse near the port in Odense.

Address; Seebladsgade 21 B, 5000 Odense C

3 Aalborg Street Food- Køkkenfabrikken

The first ongoing street food market in Aalborg is called Aalborg Street Food. Local foods and culinary experiences are highlighted here.

Address; Skudehavnsvej 35-37, 9000 Aalborg

4 Esbjerg Street Food: a variety of tasty food vendors

Discover the seven fascinating food booths at Esbjerg Street Foods, which provide delicacies to suit every palate, as well as the three bars, which have a combined 57 beer taps.

Address: Kongensgade 34, Borgergade 33, 6700 Esbjerg

5 Urbania Street Food: Eye-level fast food

Urbania is a haven where the scope pulls you inside for a fast dinner and serves as a meeting place for good times and delicious food in the city.

Address; Gothersgade 32, 7000 Fredericia

6. Vejle Street Food

There are a variety of international flavors available at Street Meal Vejle, where you may eat inside, on the patio, or take your meal home.

Address; Dmningen 44 B, 7100 Vejle

7. Copenhagen Street Food

Aarhus Street Food is a year-round street food market that offers visitors and residents alike the chance to sample a wide variety of street cuisine from more than 30 street cooks.

Address: Ny Banegaardsgade 46, 8000 Aarhus, Denmark

8. Street Food Market in Elsinore - Værftets Madmarked

The shipyard's street food market is a casual meeting place where people of all ages may congregate, enjoy, and discover the delicious delicacies found all over the globe. It features street food in a rustic, nautical setting.

Address; Ny Kronborgvej 2, Værftshallerne Hal 21, 3000 Helsingør

9. Reffen - Street Food in Copenhagen
In Refshaleen, a neighborhood in Copenhagen, Reffen is a market for organic street food and a hub for new businesses, inventions, and creativity.

Address: Refshalevej 167A, 1432 København K

10. The Kitchen at Bridge Street
The Bridge Street Kitchen, which is operated by the restaurant Noma and the Street Food District, is located in the Greenlandic Trade Square, which is directly over Inderhavsbroen (the bridge) near Nyhavn. From California Kitchen, GRD, Gasoline Grill, Pizza Bro, Kejser Sausage, Dhaba, Haddock's, Palgade, Will at the Bridge, MAC-CIK by IBU, and Barabba, you can sample top-notch street cuisine with an emphasis on organic ingredients here.

Address: Strandgade 95, 1401 Copenhagen, Denmark

Chapter 7: Must Do Things In Copenhagen

One of the most lovely towns in Northern Europe, Copenhagen is brimming with history, culture, and attractions. It's simple to spend a lot of time here exploring the many museums and opulent palaces, as well as the picturesque canal neighborhood of Nyhavn and Kongens Nytorv. Visitors are also drawn to the city's vibrant design and culinary culture. There are several art galleries, furnishing shops, fashionable boutiques, top-notch eateries, and nice cafés to warm yourself in during the chilly winter months.

These are the top attractions in Copenhagen, regardless of whether you're a first-time tourist (in which case you will undoubtedly see the most iconic monuments and maybe get a sought-after dinner reservation) or a seasoned traveler looking for more unusual experiences.

Visit Nyhavn.

The picturesque waterfront quarter of 17th-century Nyhavn, which extends from Kongens Nytorv to the harbor and is bordered by colorful townhouses and boats floating in the canals, is one of the most picturesque spots in all of Europe.

Journey in a Nordic seaplane

Getting a bird's-eye perspective of a new city is always a remarkable experience, particularly one as beautiful as Copenhagen. The concierge of Leading Hotels of the World member d'Angleterre, Cecilia Fonden, advises using a

Nordic seaplane for sightseeing. It hovers just high enough to make neighborhoods, canals, ships, beaches, and famous structures vividly visible.

Stop by CopenHill.

It is very appropriate for the Danes to build a leisure area atop a running clean energy power station. Visitors are welcome at CopenHill for hiking during the summer months and skiing throughout the winter. It is the first ski slope in Copenhagen and was skillfully built atop a municipal waste disposal facility. In the summer, visitors to this urban leisure area may go on hikes, runs, or climb the highest climbing wall in the world.

Explore Rosenborg Palace.

The gleaming crown jewels and other royal artifacts are kept at the Renaissance-era Rosenborg Castle, which was originally constructed as a summer retreat. Famously beautiful grounds surround the regal building.

Visit Kongens Have, also known as The King's Garden.

Copenhagen is renowned for its stunning public gardens and parks. Kongens Have (The King's Garden), the oldest royal garden in Denmark and the focal point of the Rosenborg Castle complex, tops the list of must-see green areas. Fonden advises taking a blanket and relaxing for a while beneath a tree in the middle of the bustling metropolis.

Explore Tivoli Gardens

With exciting rides, including one of the oldest operational wooden roller coasters, entertainment, shops, restaurants, and seasonal events, such as summer concerts and a Christmas market, the famed Tivoli Gardens is a popular and historic amusement park that is enjoyable for people of all ages.

Visit and eat at Reffen

Interested in more? Visit Reffen, the biggest Nordic location for street food. The area is home to a wide range of international booths that provide anything from Afgan lamb kebabs to shrimp barbecued in the New Orleans way. Additionally, it has bars, shops, and special events like concerts.

Port Baths

"Water surrounds Copenhagen, and on hot days, both inhabitants and tourists plunge in to cool down. All harbor baths [recreational bathing establishments] have lifeguards, some have platforms to jump from, and others have kiddie pools.

Palace of Amalienborg

Amalienborg Palace is the main house of the Danish royal family and is situated in Frederiksstaden. Queen Margrethe ll still stays there during the autumn and winter. It also has a museum where visitors may learn about a variety of fascinating facets of the monarchy. At noon, the guards will change, so be sure to watch.

Visit the canals by boat.

Taking a Hey Captain Boat across all of Copenhagen's canals may be one of the greatest ways for tourists to explore the city. "The landscape and the narrative are both stunning. Fonden said, "It's like being in a Hans-Christian Andersen story.

Rent a GoBoat.

Do you like to be the ship's captain? Hire a solar-powered, Danish-designed GoBoat and spend a few hours cruising the canals. Bring local food and drinks for a picnic to further enhance the experience.

Don't miss La Banchina

La Banchina is a well-known wine bar and walk-in restaurant that is oh-so-Copenhagen. It also has a sauna on-site and a harbor dock where you can have a cool swim.

Schedule a procedure at Amazing Space.

What would a visit to Copenhagen be without some R&R? Weary travelers may discover Amazing Space, a haven of tranquility, underneath d'Angleterre. In addition to the only indoor pool in the downtown region, the award-winning spa also provides Nordic treatments, a steam room, and a sauna.

Danish National Museum

The National Museum of Denmark is a treasure trove of Danish culture and history and is situated in the heart of the city close to many other must-see sites. It also has fascinating international exhibitions, such as African masks and Egyptian tombs. Additionally, there is a top-notch restaurant there.

Shop around Strøget.

Strøget, one of the longest pedestrian avenues in Europe and Copenhagen's renowned retail district, is the ideal location to promenade (and spend money). You may anticipate elegant stores and relaxing cafés where you can take a break from your shopping therapy excursions.

Visit Copenhagen Zoo

Considering a trip with the family to the Danish capital? More than 4,000 species from all over the globe, including giant pandas, hippopotamuses, elephants, and polar bears, may be seen at the 11-hectare (almost 30-acre) Copenhagen Zoo.

Danish National Aquarium

The National Aquarium Denmark will not fail to wow you, whether you're traveling with children or just prefer getting up close and personal with colorful aquatic life. The biggest aquarium in northern Europe is home to thousands of fish and marine life, including South American electric eels and sturgeon from Danish lakes.

Take a trip to Christiansborg Palace.

On the islet of Slotsholmen in the heart of Copenhagen, the magnificent Christiansborg Palace dates back 800 years. Currently, it serves as the location of the Danish Supreme Court, the Danish Prime Minister's Office, and the Danish Parliament.

Go to Rundetrn

Rundetrn, which was erected by King Christian IV, is undoubtedly one of Denmark's famous structures. In addition to enjoying the architecture, tourists may go to the tower observatory for breathtaking city views.

Stroll Street Jaegersborggade

The greatest stores in Copenhagen can be found on this lively street. There are 40 art galleries, antique apparel, and organic food available. Check out the ceramics shops, such as Keramiker Inge Vincents, which is renowned for its hand-shaped porcelain.

Tour Copenhagen by Foot

Due to its compact size and concentration of notable attractions in the Indre By region in the city center, Copenhagen is simple to explore on foot. There are many different types of walking tours available, from conventional tours that concentrate on the city's history to food-focused excursions with tastings and music-focused excursions with stops at jazz venues.

Our Savior's Church (Vor Frelsers Kirke)

The Church of Our Saviour in Christianshavn is among the most well-known religious locations in Denmark. Danish architect Lambert van Haven created this Palladian-style church, which was constructed in the 1680s and inaugurated in 1696. A 1698 organ, a 48-bell carillon, and an altar depicting a tableau from the New Testament are all found within. The church's oak spire, however, is its most notable feature. The spectacular spire was designed by Danish architect Lauritz de Thurah and includes a spiral staircase outside, gilded iron bars, and a gilded figure of Christ on a globe.

Ny Carlsberg Glyptotek

You will enjoy looking over the displays of Ny Carlsberg Glyptotek if you like both art and archaeology. This 1888-founded museum and research facility is home to more than 10,000 items, such as sculptures from the 19th century in France and Greek portrait heads. Paul Gauguin, a post-impressionist painter, is shown here, as is Auguste Rodin, a sculptor.

Hire a bike

One of the world's bike-friendliest cities has to be Copenhagen. Almost everyone who lives here commutes by bicycle daily, and since it's so safe, you'll often see individuals riding without helmets. People are urged to pedal whenever they need to go since cycling reduces pollution, which is helped by the fact that the city is flat. In Copenhagen, several businesses provide rentals, but you may want to check out the cutting-edge City Bike program, which has been in operation since 1995.

The Collection of David

Check out the Danish millionaire C.L.'s private art collection here. The building, David, who also contributed the artwork, as well as his old residence and the biggest collection of Islamic art in Scandinavia. Additionally, there are displays of European art from the 18th century as well as Danish contemporary art and paintings from the Danish Golden Age of the 19th century. The Islamic area is the main draw, including beautiful objects that date from the 800s to the 1800s and were collected from Spain to India. Although calligraphy is dominant, there are also lovely glass and ceramic objects in this shop. The attraction offers free admission.

Bakken Family Fun Center

Bakken is an entertainment park that has been present since 1583 and offers a rustic substitute for Tivoli Gardens. This makes it the world's longest continuously operational amusement park, as you would have guessed. The second-most visited tourist destination in Denmark, after Tivoli Gardens, is Bakken, which is tucked away in a beech forest a few kilometers north of Copenhagen. Bakken's attractions have a nostalgic, vintage feel to them, including Rutschebanen with its rickety wooden scaffold from 1932 or the cabaret-hosting Hvile music hall. The park is free to enter, but you must purchase a ticket for each ride.

Immerse Yourself In High-Quality Design

What better location to get up close and personal with these renowned works of simplicity and functionalism than at the Designmuseum Danmark? Danish Design is a functionalistic design and architectural style that sprang from the German Bauhaus movement. A must-see and very unusual museum with a chic café and lovely store where you can buy yourself some Danish industrial design trinkets.

With Kayak, View the City in a New Light

Over the last several decades, Copenhagen's Harbour has undergone an almost complete transformation and is now a secure area to explore (and swim)! Why not think about renting a kayak for individuals who want a little bit more excitement than a standard harbor trip and wish to lessen their carbon footprint? You are free to explore on your own or with a guided tour; several businesses hire them out.

Visit the Kastrup Sea Baths and have a dip

One of Copenhagen's restad district's numerous architectural gems is the Kastrup Sea Bath.

Kastrup Sea Bath has transformed this abandoned brownfield site into one of Copenhagen's most alluring, immediately identifiable, and prosperous leisure attractions. It was created as a contemporary outdoor swimming facility for the general public.

Show respect for the your kings and queens at Roskilde Cathedral

Okay, so this isn't really one of the nicest things to do "in" Copenhagen, but because I was traveling with the Copenhagen Card, it was simple to get there and free admission was available. Furthermore, the Roskilde Cathedral is listed as a World Heritage Site by UNESCO, so you should see it!

Hear, See, And Feel Music History at RAGNAROCK

Since I've already persuaded you to go to Roskilde, you must also not miss this incredible museum that was only recently established and is devoted to Danish music. It explores the influence of Danish music on society and how young people have used it to create their own culture and rebelliousness. The Copenhagen Card also grants free admission.

Visit The Royal Copenhagen Flagship Store To Take In Centuries Of History

Visit here to look through Royal Copenhagen's historical treasures, which are currently among the most visited tourist destinations in Copenhagen. Their plates, cases, cups, mugs, bowls, teapots, and other items are wonderful keepsakes that can last a lifetime if your budget allows. I learned that while their signature blue-and-white porcelain is now produced in Thailand, 15 craftspeople still work in Denmark to create their Flora Danica floral line.

At the Politikens Boghal Bookstore, indulge your inner bookworm

This two-store shrine to literature, which is conveniently situated in the city's heart right off City Hall Square, has a rich and storied history. Politiken, one of Denmark's leading newspapers, formerly called the structure home. However, it was given fresh life in 1915 when it became a tiny bookshop. Just a few years later, it was split into local and international divisions, continuing the pattern.

Experience The Elegant Copenhagen Opera House

The Danish people received the National Opera House in Copenhagen as a gift from shipping tycoon A.P. in 2001. Møller. Along with Sydney and Oslo, it is among the world's most cutting-edge opera houses and one of the most stunning I've ever seen.

Explore The Stunning Danish Architecture Center

This is where architecture, design, and urban culture in Denmark convene most often. The mission and objective of the Danish Architecture Center are to promote interaction between architects and the building industry.

Expect The Unexpected At Cisternerne

Cisternerne is a unique, subterranean exhibition venue that is both beautiful and eerie. a setting where art integrates with the surrounding surroundings.

Visit The Huset-KBH Culture House Copenhagen To Meet Locals

The first and biggest cultural house in Denmark, Huset-KBH (or simply "Huset"), was founded in 1970. It is housed in a separate former warehouse as well as three historic townhouses.

Admire the 400-year-old royal artwork and treasures at Rosenborg Castle.

Castles and palaces abound throughout Denmark. However, what makes the Rosenborg Castle unique are the items kept there, which highlight royal Danish culture from the late 16th to 19th centuries rather than just another one of Christian IV's many architectural creations or in the Flemish Renaissance style.

Relax With A Film At Cinematek

The national center for Danish Cinema, where you may see movies, browse the bookstore, or have a snack in the on-site café after a movie. Each month, more than 70 movies are shown in the Cinematheque's three theaters, many of which have English or English subtitles.

Visit Sweden for a day trip and Explore Neighboring Countries (Lund & Malmö)

One of Copenhagen's many benefits is its excellent location as a starting point for experiencing more stunning Scandinavia. Take, for instance, this wonderful day excursion to the Swedish cities of Lund and Malmö. You're leaving the city for the day, but you're also leaving the nation for the day, that's right!

These two towns are included in the Greater Copenhagen area since they are so near to the Danish capital. You can reach Lund, an ancient Viking settlement still containing many of its Rune Stones, by taking a short bus journey over the magnificent refund bridge.

Wonder at Wooden Skyscraper

This unusual building in the middle of a Danish woodland was named one of the top tourist destinations in the world by TIME Magazine. You'll understand why after you see it. An observation tower called The Wooden Skyscraper resembles something out of a fairy tale.

A spiral path that offers views of the surrounding landscape from every imaginable height and angle is made possible by the strikingly curved design. This is the ideal location for amateur (or expert!) photographers because of the breathtaking surroundings.

Chapter 8: Copenhagen Christmas Celebration And Markets

Christmas Celebration

Experiencing the Christmas celebrations in Copenhagen:

1. Festive Atmosphere:

Copenhagen embraces the holiday spirit with elaborate decorations, lights, and festive displays throughout the city. The streets, parks, and landmarks are adorned with twinkling lights, creating a magical ambiance.

2. Christmas Markets:

Explore various Christmas markets offering crafts, gifts, decorations, and traditional Danish foods. The Tivoli Gardens Christmas Market is a must-visit, with its enchanting atmosphere, rides, and entertainment. Nyhavn's waterfront market and the medieval-themed market at Kronborg Castle are also popular options, many more markets.

3. Culinary Delights:

Indulge in Danish Christmas specialties like "æbleskiver" (round pancakes), "gløgg" (mulled wine), and "pebernødder" (spiced cookies). Try "flæskesteg" (roast pork) or "risengrød" (rice pudding) — traditional dishes often enjoyed during the season.

4. Events and Activities:

Attend Christmas concerts, carol services, and special performances held at various venues, including churches and cultural centers. Ice skating rinks pop up in different parts of the city, offering a fun way to enjoy the winter weather.

5. Christmas Eve Traditions:

Christmas Eve (December 24th) is the main celebration day in Denmark. Many locals gather for a festive meal, exchange gifts, and dance around the Christmas tree. Experience the traditional "Julefrokost" (Christmas lunch) with family or friends, featuring a spread of Danish delicacies.

6. Church Services:

Attend a Christmas church service at one of Copenhagen's historic churches, such as the Copenhagen Cathedral or Church of Our Lady. Midnight Mass is a special tradition on Christmas Eve.

7. Santa Lucia Day:

Celebrated on December 13th, this Swedish tradition is also observed in Copenhagen. Young girls dressed in white and wearing crowns of candles process through the city singing traditional songs.

8. New Year's Eve:

Copenhagen hosts a grand New Year's Eve celebration with fireworks at the iconic Tivoli Gardens and around the harbor. Locals often gather in city squares to celebrate the arrival of the new year.

9. Shopping and Gifts:

Copenhagen's shopping districts, such as Strøget, offer a variety of boutiques, department stores, and designer shops for holiday shopping.

10. Winter Walks and Sightseeing:

Take leisurely winter walks along the canals, through historic neighborhoods, and by iconic landmarks like the Little Mermaid statue.

11. Practical Tips:

Dress warmly, as Copenhagen can be quite cold during the winter months. Check the opening hours and specific dates for Christmas markets, events, and attractions in advance

Christmas Markets In Copenhagen

Here's a comprehensive guide to Copenhagen's Christmas markets, along with their approximate opening and closing dates:

Tips:

Opening times: 11am to 10pm and until midnight on the weekends.

Christmas Day: The markets are closed on 24, 25 and 26 December.

Admission: Tivoli requires purchasing a ticket and the other Christmas markets are free.

Santa: Yes, on most days.

Ice skating: Yes, at Tivoli Gardens and Frederiksberg Gardens.

Vegetarian: Yes, plenty of options.

Vegan: Yes, plenty of options.

Gluten free: Yes, but limited.

Accessible: Yes, if you can manage cobblestones.

Pet-friendly: Yes, dogs are allowed on a lead.

Recommended tour: Hygge and Happiness Culture Tour

Copenhagen weather in winter: Temperatures average 5°C / 1°C (high / low) in December.

Tivoli Gardens Christmas Market:

Dates: November 17–December 31, 2023
Description: Tivoli Gardens, one of the world's oldest amusement parks, transforms into a festive wonderland. Enjoy enchanting lights, holiday decorations, traditional Danish treats, and rides. Check the Tivoli Gardens website for exact dates.

Nyhavn Christmas Market:

Dates: Mid-November to late December
Description: Nyhavn's charming waterfront hosts stalls selling holiday goodies, crafts, and ornaments. The festive atmosphere is perfect for a leisurely stroll and a cup of warm gløgg (mulled wine).

Højbro Plads Christmas Market:

Dates: November 17–December 31, 2023
Description: Located in the heart of the city, this market offers a mix of traditional and

modern holiday items. Explore the various stalls featuring crafts, clothing, and delicious seasonal treats.

Kongens Nytorv Christmas Market:

Dates: November 17–December 21, 2023
Description: This market, situated near Nyhavn, boasts an elegant setting and high-quality goods. Discover unique crafts, decorations, and culinary delights as you soak in the festive atmosphere.

Copenhagen Christmas Market at Kronborg Castle:

Dates: Late November to mid-December
Description: Take a short trip from Copenhagen to the Kronborg Castle for a historical Christmas market. Explore the stalls within the castle walls, enjoy traditional entertainment, and experience the magic of the season.

Copenhagen Designer Christmas Market:

Dates: Early to mid-December
Description: This market features local designers and artisans showcasing their unique creations. Find special gifts and crafts in an intimate setting that celebrates craftsmanship and creativity.

Christmas Market at Axeltorv:

Dates: Early to mid-December
Description: This smaller market in Nørrebro offers a cozy and inviting atmosphere. Browse through handcrafted goods, savor local treats, and embrace the holiday spirit.

Hans Christian Andersen Christmas Market:

Dates: November- December
Description: This market is inspired by the fairy tales of the famous Danish author, Hans

Christian Andersen. It's a smaller market but offers a selection of crafts and festive goodies.

Frederiksberg Christmas Market:

Dates: November- December
Description: In the courtyard of Frederiksberg Palace, this market showcases Danish crafts, gifts, and food. The palace itself provides a grand backdrop to the festivities.

Paper Island Christmas Market:

Dates: November- December
Description: Known for its street food, Paper Island (Papirøen) hosts a special Christmas market. Explore unique gifts, artwork, and handmade items while savoring delicious street food options.

Christmas in Taastrup:

Dates: November- December
Description; Just outside Copenhagen, the Christmas market in Taastrup offers a traditional atmosphere with stalls, entertainment, and seasonal treats. It's a cozy option for a festive outing.

Islands Brygge Christmas Market:

Dates: November- December
Description: This local market is perfect for families. It features a cozy atmosphere with stalls offering handmade gifts, sweets, and warm drinks. There's often entertainment for children as well.

Remember that dates may vary slightly from year to year, so it's a good idea to check the official websites or local event listings closer to the time of your visit. Bundle up in warm clothing and enjoy the enchanting Christmas markets that Copenhagen has to offer!

Chapter 9; Nightlife In Copenhagen

Experience the vibrant nightlife of Copenhagen:

1. Diverse Nightlife Scene:

Copenhagen offers a diverse range of nightlife options, from trendy bars to live music venues, nightclubs, and cultural events.

2. Nightclubs and Dance Venues

The Meatpacking District (Kødbyen) is a hub of nightlife, featuring popular nightclubs like Jolene, KB18, and Bakken. Culture Box is a renowned techno and electronic music venue, attracting international DJs and music enthusiasts.

3. Live Music Venues:

Vega hosts live concerts by both local and international artists, covering a variety of genres. Loppen, situated in Christiania, is a unique venue with an eclectic lineup of bands and performers.

4. Bars and Pubs:

Explore the bar scene in Vesterbro and Nørrebro neighborhoods, where you'll find cozy pubs, cocktail bars, and local hangouts. Try Mikkeller Bar for a wide selection of craft beers or Ruby for expertly crafted cocktails.

5. Jazz and Blues:

Copenhagen has a rich jazz heritage. Visit Jazzhus Montmartre for classic jazz performances or La Fontaine for a more intimate jazz experience.

6. Canal Cruises:

Enjoy Copenhagen's waterfront in a unique way by taking a canal cruise at night. Some tours offer dinner and drinks on board.

7. Nighttime Tours and Experiences:

Consider joining a guided nighttime bike tour or a walking tour to explore the city's illuminated landmarks and hidden gems.

8. Street Food and Late-Night Eats:

Try Reffen Street Food Market for a variety of international dishes, or visit traditional Danish eateries that offer late-night snacks.

9. LGBTQ+ Nightlife:

Copenhagen is known for its LGBTQ+-friendly atmosphere. Head to places like Oscar Bar Café and G-A-Y Copenhagen for LGBTQ+ nightlife.

10. Special Events and Festivals:

Check out the city's event calendar for special nightlife events, festivals, and themed parties happening during your visit.

11. Practical Tips:

Many places have a cover charge, especially on weekends. The legal drinking age is 18, and IDs may be required for entry. Public transportation is available throughout the night, making it easy to get around.

Night Activities

Night activities in Copenhagen, offering a wide range of options to suit various preferences:

Stroll through Illuminated Landmarks:
Take a leisurely walk through the city and admire iconic landmarks beautifully

illuminated at night, such as the Tivoli Gardens, Christiansborg Palace, and the Marble Church.

Attend Evening Performances:
Catch a live performance at venues like the Royal Danish Theatre or the Opera House. Experience ballet, theater, opera, and musical performances.

Enjoy Live Music:
Immerse yourself in Copenhagen's vibrant music scene. Check out jazz performances at venues like Jazzhus Montmartre or rock out to live bands at Vega.

Night Photography Tours:
Join a night photography tour to capture stunning shots of Copenhagen's landmarks illuminated against the dark sky.

Midnight Bike Ride:

Copenhagen is a cycling-friendly city. Rent a bike and enjoy a peaceful midnight ride through the quiet streets.

Night Markets and Fairs:

Keep an eye out for night markets, craft fairs, and special events offering unique shopping experiences and local goods.

Late-Night Dining:

Savor late-night dining at restaurants and eateries that stay open. Try traditional Danish dishes or international cuisines.

Star Gazing at the Planetarium:

Visit the Tycho Brahe Planetarium to learn about astronomy and marvel at the starry night sky in the planetarium dome.

Visit Christiania:

Explore the alternative neighborhood of Christiania at night. Experience its unique atmosphere, art installations, and cafes.

Attend Nighttime Events:
Look out for special nighttime events, exhibitions, and cultural activities happening across the city.

Evening Park Walks:
Take a relaxing evening stroll in parks like King's Garden or Ørstedsparken, and enjoy the tranquil surroundings.

Quiet Moments by the Waterfront:
Sit by the waterfront, relax, and watch the lights shimmering on the water. The peaceful atmosphere can be truly rejuvenating.

Remember to check the opening hours and any special events before heading out. Copenhagen offers an array of nighttime activities that cater to various interests, ensuring you have an unforgettable experience in the Danish capital after the sun sets

Chapter 10: Copenhagen For Solo Travelers

Surviving Tip*s*:
-*You can save money on your trip to Copenhagen as a solo traveler with the **Copenhagen Card**, which includes free admission to 89+ attractions and activities.*

-*Copenhagen is safe for solo travel however its still smart to pack travel safety essentials. Like **She's Birdie Personal Safety Alarm,** which can help scare away potential attackers and it's TSA-approved. Another one is **Clever Travel Companion Pickpocket-Proof Garments**. The other one is **Speakeasy Travel Supply Hidden Pocket Scarves**

Planning Your Trip:

Best Time to Visit: Late spring to early autumn (May to September) is ideal for pleasant weather.

Visa Requirements: Check if you need a visa before you travel.

Accommodation: Book a centrally located hotel, hostel, or Airbnb.

Solo Activities:

Explore Nyhavn: Stroll along the picturesque harbor, enjoy the colorful buildings, and maybe take a canal cruise.

Visit Tivoli Gardens: An amusement park in the heart of the city with rides, beautiful gardens, and entertainment.

Discover The Little Mermaid: See the iconic statue inspired by Hans Christian Andersen's fairy tale.

Bike Tour: Copenhagen is a bike-friendly city, so rent a bike and explore its many cycle lanes and scenic routes.

Food Market Visit: Explore Torvehallerne or Paper Island for a variety of Danish and international foods.

Rosenborg Castle: Explore this 17th-century royal castle and its impressive collection of artifacts.

Christiania: Visit this unique self-governing neighborhood known for its artistic atmosphere and alternative lifestyle.

National Museum of Denmark: Immerse yourself in Danish history and culture through its impressive exhibits.

Boat Tours: Enjoy a relaxing boat ride along the canals.

Walking Tours: Join guided tours to explore the city's history and hidden gems.

Copenhagen Free Walking Tours: Budget-friendly tours led by locals.

Visit The Open Air Museum (Frilandsmuseet);
This Museum is a good attraction for solo travelers to Copenhagen who want to immerse themselves in history and Danish culture.

Spend A Day At Bakken Amusement Park.

Tours for Solo Travelers In Copenhagen

The Copenhagen Culinary Experience Food Tour

3-Hour Copenhagen City Highlights Bike Tour

Copenhagen Canal Cruise

Vesterbro Cultural Tour with Beer Tasting

Highlights & Secrets Of Copenhagen

Malmö & Lund Tour: Crossing the Bridge to Sweden

Copenhagen Pub Crawl

Classic Canal Tour With Live Guide.

Best Area to Stay For Solo Travelers:

Indre By (City Center): Offers easy access to major attractions, shopping, and dining.

Vesterbro: Known for its trendy boutiques, cafes, and lively nightlife.

Nørrebro: A diverse neighborhood with hipster vibes, street art, and multicultural food options.

Frederiksberg: Offers a more residential feel with parks and a zoo, and it's still close to the city center.

Osterbro: A quiet and upscale area with beautiful parks and waterfront views.

Culinary Delights:

Smørrebrød: Traditional open-faced sandwiches.

New Nordic Cuisine: Explore innovative dishes at fine dining restaurants.

Street Food Markets: Visit Paper Island (Papirøen) or Reffen for diverse food stalls.

For something traditional, visit Restaurant Puk Or Restaurant Kronborg.

For unforgettable meals, visit Restaurant Palægade Or Møntergade.

Chapter 11: Things To Avoid In Copenhagen

Any new destination is intriguing to visit since it offers a variety of interesting attractions and cultural experiences that can quickly become overwhelming. However, even if the idea of visiting Copenhagen, Denmark's energetic capital city, might be immensely alluring, it's crucial to keep in mind that a few missteps could easily spoil your plans.

If you're only planning a trip to Copenhagen, you'll want to make the most of your time there. Despite the abundance of sights and activities in this lovely city, some things could easily ruin your trip. Here is a list of things to keep away from during your visit to Copenhagen.

Lack of Planning; While a quick trip to Copenhagen can be thrilling, it's crucial to conduct your homework and compile a list of things to do in Copenhagen while you're there. You risk missing out on many of the major attractions in the city if you don't.

One of the most crucial things to keep in mind when visiting any city is to be well-prepared and avoid getting lost. Take a map or learn how to navigate about. The easiest approach to accomplish this in Copenhagen is to be prepared with a map and an awareness of the city's layout. Learn about all the important sites and any locations you can visit while there.

Forgetting To Compare Different Currency Exchange Rates: Rather than picking a company at random, one of the greatest methods to ensure you obtain the best exchange rate is to look for recognized companies that offer competitive rates. Before leaving, find out which locations in Copenhagen give the best exchange rates and make a note of their locations.

Overstaying Or Underestimating Your Visa Requirements; Before visiting Copenhagen, make sure you are aware of the visa requirements for your home country. You might require a separate visa, which could include various processes and paperwork, depending on your nation.

Not budgeting for travel and hotel expenses can make a trip to Copenhagen rather expensive. In addition to the typical high cost of lodging, travel expenses and admission fees can start to mount. A City Pass, which offers discounts on admission prices as well as other attractions in the city, is a worthwhile investment if you want to save money.

Additionally, do some research in advance on lodging options, such as hotels, and seek for any available discounts. Making reservations in advance can also enable you to avoid unforeseen expenses. If you intend to drive, don't forget to account for the expense of parking or gas.

Being careless with safety precautions or unaware of potential pickpockets and scams; It's crucial to remain alert of potential frauds and pickpockets while visiting Copenhagen. Your most priceless possessions should never be kept in plain sight; instead, they should be kept in safe places.

Visitation During The Wrong Season: A little trip to Copenhagen can be ruined by visiting during the incorrect season! Although Copenhagen is renowned for having moderate weather all year round, some months will have fewer daylight hours and more erratic rainfall than others.

Going Out At Night Without Knowing Where ; Can Ruin Your Visit To Copenhagen! Even though the city has a thriving nightlife, there are several places you should stay away from to keep yourself safe.

Jaywalking: Copenhagen is known for its cycling culture, and pedestrians should be careful when crossing the streets to avoid disrupting the flow of cyclists.

Blocking bike lanes: Be mindful not to stand or walk in bike lanes, as cyclists use them as their main mode of transportation.

Ignoring traffic signals: Always follow traffic signals and pedestrian crossings to ensure your safety and the smooth flow of traffic.

Excessive noise: Danes value peace and quiet, so avoid being excessively loud, especially in residential areas and public transportation.

Public intoxication: While enjoying the city's nightlife, remember that public intoxication is frowned upon and can lead to disturbances or legal issues.

Smoking in restricted areas: Copenhagen has strict smoking regulations. Avoid smoking in enclosed public spaces, restaurants, and certain outdoor areas where smoking is prohibited.

Littering: Copenhagen is known for its cleanliness. Dispose of trash properly in designated bins to help maintain the city's pristine environment.

Taking photos of people without permission: It's polite to ask for permission before taking photos of locals, especially in intimate or personal situations.

Over-tipping: Tipping is not as common in Denmark as in other countries. While it's not discouraged, it's not obligatory either. Check if service charges are included in your bill before tipping.

Disregarding cultural norms: Respect local customs and traditions. For instance, don't interrupt or engage in small talk with strangers unless it's appropriate.

Disrespecting personal space: Danes value their personal space. Avoid standing too close to others in queues, on public transportation, or in public places.

Ignoring bike etiquette: If you decide to rent a bike, familiarize yourself with cycling rules and etiquette to ensure a safe and enjoyable experience for everyone.

Not Using Cashless Payment: Denmark is largely a cashless society. Avoid carrying too much cash and make use of credit/debit cards or mobile payment apps.

Being Impatient at Cafés: Danish cafés encourage leisurely enjoyment. Avoid rushing through your meal or drink; take your time and savor the experience.

Not Visiting During Peak Seasons: While peak seasons can be crowded, some attractions and events might be closed during off-peak times. Avoid missing out by planning your visit accordingly.

Ignoring the Weather: Copenhagen weather can be unpredictable. Avoid being caught unprepared by checking the forecast and dressing appropriately.

Expecting 24/7 Shopping: Shops in Copenhagen might close earlier than you're used to, especially on weekends. Avoid disappointment by checking the opening hours in advance.

Skipping Reservations: Copenhagen's popular restaurants can get fully booked quickly. Avoid disappointment by making reservations in advance.

Overpriced Tourist Traps: Some restaurants and shops in touristy areas might be expensive. Look for local recommendations for more authentic and budget-friendly options.

Chapter 12: Samples Of Planned Itineraries

One of the finest choices you can make is to go to Copenhagen. You will undoubtedly enjoy your vacation.

But how long is best to spend in Copenhagen?

This is a general question that could be answered very much anywhere in the globe, not just in Copenhagen. How many? I believe that as a full-time traveler, I have developed the capacity to evaluate this subject rather effectively. How many days in Copenhagen is enough? is a question I feel confident answering after visiting the Danish capital.

So let's get started right now!

I stayed in Copenhagen for three days, and I think that's the ideal length of time.

Therefore, I believe that three days is a sufficient amount of time to spend in Copenhagen. Despite this, everyone has varied preferences about the number of activities to do in a day, the amount of downtime, etc.

Copenhagen may certainly be seen in two days and even in one, but at least three days is required to experience the city, visit all the major sights, and have time to unwind or explore the area.

I was able to explore all the major sights during my three days in Copenhagen, some of them more than once, and I had plenty of free time to live like a local, which is a pretty peaceful and laid-back lifestyle. You may visit Copenhagen with confidence since it is both the safest and one of the happiest cities in the world.

Naturally, you may extend your stay in Copenhagen and still enjoy yourself. There are always more than enough days in Copenhagen since there are so many hidden treasures to discover there.

Sample Of 3 Days Planned Itinerary

Here is a quick summary of my trip.

Day 1: Nyhavn and canal tour, Frederiksberg Palace, Christiansborg Palace, and Copenhagen Zoo.

Since the zoo was my first stop on my vacation to Copenhagen, I went there first thing in the morning before it opened at 10 a.m. I also went to Frederiksberg Palace when I was outside of Copenhagen since it is just next to the zoo. I afterward returned to Copenhagen's city center, where I went to Christiansborg Palace and climbed the tower for a lovely perspective of the area.

You should also visit Nyhavn, Copenhagen's most well-known attraction, on your first day there. It's worth taking a canal trip here as well since it's really attractive to look at and where most canal excursions start and conclude. Day 1 also includes it since it will include viewing the Opera House.

Day 2: Bicycle Tour, Tivoli Gardens, Rosenborg Castle, and the Round Tower.

I went on a bike tour around Copenhagen to start my second day there. This is also included in Day 2 since it covers most of the major attractions, including the Little Mermaid. After that, I went to Rosenborg Castle and saw the museums. Best Practice: The Copenhagen Card gives you free admission to the majority of the tourist sites.

I climbed The Round Tower to get another stunning perspective of Copenhagen before going to Tivoli Gardens in the evening to see it all lit up. It has one of the most beautiful skylines I've ever seen, and it's different from skyscrapers like those in cities like London to see spires instead.

Day 3: Carlsberg Brewery, Amelianborg, and the National Museum.

Start your last day in Copenhagen with a visit to Amelianborg; both the exterior and the interior are exquisite. The last day of the three days is off to a wonderful start. After that, I went to the National Museum to learn more about Danish and Scandinavian history. It was an excellent experience and extremely informative.

The Carlsberg Brewery was the final thing I saw in Copenhagen. As you can see, I visited various places throughout my three days that some people would not deem necessary. The major attractions in Copenhagen may be seen in two days or even one day, as I previously said.

Sample Of 5 Days Planned Itinerary
Day 1

I couldn't wait to start my plan for Copenhagen after arriving at Copenhagen Airport! There are various ways to get to the city center, including using the metro, a cab, or renting a vehicle. You can't go wrong since they are all excellent possibilities. Just be aware that it will cost more to get there than normal! You'll quickly find yourself in the center of the Danish capital. Let's get started with your first day in this beautiful city.

1. Explore the Kastellet.

The point is, you won't even need to go far to begin taking advantage of all this lovely city has to offer. Just across the street from the hotel is the Kastellet and its adjacent park. This ancient fortification is a wonderful location for a stroll as well as a fantastic method to learn about Copenhagen's history. You'll enjoy getting lost in the thick vegetation and taking in the beautiful scenery.

2. Explore City Hall Square.

Visit City Hall Square, one of the greatest locations to immerse oneself in the center of the Danish city, after touring Kastellet. Make sure to stop at the Little Yellow Coffee Bar for a coffee to fuel your exploration as you stroll around the busy area. Nearby, there are several well-known landmarks, including:

3. Enjoy a Pescatarian dinner.

The Michelin-starred restaurant Pecatarian is the place to go if you want to spend. You must go to this seafood restaurant, which is just next to Hotel Babette Guldsmeden, for a feast you won't soon forget. Each dish on their multi-course tasting menu is expertly created, showcasing the freshest local fresh seafood.

Day 2

1. Experience the hotel's spa, Babette Guldsmeden.; On your second day in Copenhagen, Denmark, get up and shine! The

spa at Hotel Babette Guldsmeden is the perfect place to unwind before your day begins. You'll like the serene atmosphere of the spa and sauna, which is ideal for relaxing and getting ready for another day of excursions in the Danish city. What's best? Use the spa's happy hour as an opportunity to treat yourself without spending a fortune. Also, hotel guests are welcome to use it! So be sure to there early in the morning to avoid the throng and have some peaceful time to yourself.

2. Visit the Canals from Nyhavn; After leaving the spa feeling revitalized, it's time to see Copenhagen from a new angle. Get on a canal cruise by going to Nyhavn. The good news is that you can pay for this amazing event with your Copenhagen Card! That's true, there's no need to shell out more money for this essential exercise.

3. Lunch at Havfruen Restaurant ; You'll almost doubt work up an appetite as you continue to tour the locations on your schedule for Copenhagen. One of the nicest spots to get a meal in the heart of the city is Restaurant

Havfruen. This lovely restaurant serves a variety of delectable seafood meals with some of the freshest fresh fish in the area.

It's impossible to go wrong with a Hugo and a bowl of fish soup. This combination is a culinary marriage made in heaven! Prosecco, elderflower syrup, seltzer, and mint leaves are the main ingredients of the famous drink known as Hugo. The fish soup has a hearty tomato broth, flaky, delicate fish, and spices. It will provide you with the energy you need to continue your excursions in the Danish capital.

4. Learn more about Christiansborg Palace; You should visit the majestic Christiansborg Palace if you are interested in learning about the history of the Danish royal family. You'll be astounded by the magnificent architecture and rich tradition of this spectacular monument as part of your agenda for Copenhagen. And what's this? You may get free entrance with your Copenhagen Card! Yes, there is no need to spend more funds.

5. Christiansborg Palace's Queen's Library.; You may learn about the royal Danish lifestyle while touring the palace and taking in its lavish decor. You'll feel as if you've walked into a storybook, from the opulent Royal Reception Rooms to the Great Hall with its breathtaking tapestries. That's not all, however. For an even richer experience, don't forget to explore the palace's underground ruins and the royal stables.

5. Dine at Amalia's Restaurant; You merit a meal fit for a king after a day of exploring! Restaurant Amalie fills that need. This Michelin Star restaurant is the ideal place to treat your palate to the best of Danish cuisine. You won't be let down.

A culinary work of art, Restaurant Amalie's menu offers delectable dishes made from top-quality, regional ingredients. It's the perfect place for a special evening out because of the ambiance, which is elegant but warm. Additionally, the knowledgeable staff will be happy to guide you through the menu if you need some professional advice.

Day 3

1. brunch at St. Bageri, Peders ; Your third day in Copenhagen will be busy but exciting! You'll begin the day by going to the city's oldest bakery, Sct. Bageri Peders. It's a must for first-time visitors to Copenhagen! What's so special about it, you ask? They offer a wide array of unique Danish pastries and bread including their famous "Onsdagssnegl" (Wednesday Snail) cinnamon rolls that come with your choice of white frosting or powdered sugar.

2. Spend the Day at Tivoli Gardens; Ready for some amusement park fun? Tivoli Gardens is next on your Copenhagen itinerary, and it's hands-down one of the most popular attractions in the city. This iconic amusement park has been delighting visitors since 1843, and it's not hard to see why!

Once you step inside, you'll be swept away by the enchanting atmosphere. With its beautiful gardens, charming old-world rides, and modern thrillers, there's something for everyone here. Whether you're a first-timer or a seasoned amusement park aficionado, you'll find plenty to keep you entertained.

3. Have dinner at Madklubben Vesterbro; When the sun goes down, head to Madklubben Vesterbro for an upscale Danish meal. This trendy spot is perfect for capping off your day of exploration, and it's just a short walk from Tivoli Gardens!

Day 4

Your Day 4 is all about exploring beyond the city limits. The great thing about Copenhagen is that it's the perfect launchpad for some amazing day trips. With the city's efficient public transport and well-connected metro stations, you'll find it easy to venture out and discover the beautiful places surrounding the Danish capital. In no time at all, you'll find yourself immersed in the charm of Northern Europe, with stunning landscapes and quaint towns just a short train ride away.

1. Take a day tour of Sweden; Embark on a day tour to Sweden and experience the magic of two countries in one trip. A popular choice

among visitors is the full-day tour to Lund and Malmö in Sweden, with plenty of time to explore these charming cities before returning to Copenhagen in the late afternoon. You can book this tour through Viator with many options for departure times and dates.

Lund is a picturesque university town that boasts beautiful architecture and a rich history. Stroll through the cobblestone streets, and don't miss the stunning Lund Cathedral, a true testament to the town's medieval roots. You'll be amazed by the beauty and culture this small town has to offer.

2. Grab Dinner at Aamanns 1921; After returning from your unforgettable Swedish day tour, enjoy a hearty Danish meal to wrap up the day at the Danish culinary gem of Aamanns 1921. This trendy restaurant, nestled in the city center is renowned for its art-worthy smørrebrød and contemporary cuisine. With a modern twist on classic Danish dishes, Aamann's 1921 has transformed the way smørrebrød is perceived and enjoyed. The staff even gathers the herbs for their snaps and menu

items themselves. Trust me, you'll want to add this to your Copenhagen itinerary!

3. Drinks at Library Bar; After indulging in a smørrebrød at Aamanns 1921, sip some classic cocktails at the iconic Library Bar in Copenhagen Plaza. This sophisticated yet cozy bar takes you back to a bygone era with its Chesterfield armchairs, and noble portraits adorning paneled walls. It's also home to endless rows of leather-bound books – including several first editions!

At the Library Bar, you'll find a fantastic selection of champagnes, cognacs, whiskies, and of course, some of the best cocktails in the city. While you're soaking in the ambiance, don't forget to ask the passionate bartenders for their recommendations.

Day 5
This one's for you lucky folks without an early morning flight, giving you extra time to explore more of the city on your Copenhagen itinerary.

1. Grab breakfast at Ø2; Kick off your day with a delicious breakfast at Ø2. They don't take reservations, but they're open 365 days a year, so you're in luck! Treat yourself to their famous avocado toast, fluffy pancakes, or an energizing smoothie bowl. No matter what you order, it will be the perfect start to your final day in Copenhagen.

2. Admire Art at the Ny Carlsberg Glyptotek; Once you're feeling fueled up, head over to the Ny Carlsberg Glyptotek to admire some incredible art. This stunning museum houses an impressive collection of ancient sculptures, as well as paintings by renowned artists like Van Gogh and Gauguin. You'll be mesmerized by the beautiful surroundings – don't forget to check out the lovely Winter Garden!

3. Explore the city one last time; Take this opportunity to revisit your favorite spots or discover new ones. Wander through the city center, pop into that cute boutique you noticed earlier, or savor a delicious Danish pastry at a cozy café. Copenhagen is home to more than half a dozen Danish palaces – four of which are

right in the city center! Make the most of your last hours in this beautiful place!

4. Head back to the airport; Time flies when you're having fun, but after you finish exploring, it will be time to head back to Copenhagen Airport. Be sure to arrive a few hours before departure for an international flight. Arrive four hours early during the summer months or if you need to return a rental car. The airport can get crowded, and those check-in lines can be long. Better safe than sorry!

In case you fancy a scenic road trip, driving to Copenhagen is a great way to explore the Danish countryside. From Germany, it's a 7-hour drive via the Fehmarn Belt Fixed Link, while from Sweden, you can cross the Öresund Bridge in just 45 minutes.

Printed in Great Britain
by Amazon

28373137R00116